PRESTON COTTON MARTYRS

A PLAN

OF THE

BOROUGH TOWN OF PRESTON

in the

County of Lancaster

From an actual Survey by Wm. Shakeshaft
in the Year 1809 Now republished with
Alterations
Laid down under the direction
Wm. MILLER JUNE 18

Scale of ⅜ of a Mile

Preston Cotton Martyrs

The millworkers who shocked a nation

J. S. Leigh

Palatine Books, 2007

Preston Cotton Martyrs: The millworkers who shocked a nation

Copyright © J. S. Leigh, 2008

First published in 2008 by Palatine Books,
an imprint of Carnegie Publishing
Carnegie House, Chatsworth Road, Lancaster LA1 4SL
www.palatinebooks.com

ISBN 978-1-874181-45-3

British Library Cataloguing-in-Publication data
A catalogue record for this book is available from the British Library

Designed and typeset by Carnegie Book Production, Lancaster
Printed and bound by Alden Press, Oxford

Frontispiece: A detail of Shakeshaft's map of Preston, based on a survey of 1809 and updated to the year 1822. This important early map shows Preston amid the crucial first phase of industrialisation as the town was transformed from a genteel Georgian market town into one of the country's most infamous industrial towns.
BY KIND PERMISSION OF THE COUNTY ARCHIVIST, LANCASHIRE RECORD OFFICE

Contents

In memory of my parents
William Leigh (1923–2001)
Beatrice Leigh (1923–1992)

ALSO

my aunt Martha (1905–78),
who worked for forty-eight years within Preston's cotton mills

AND

the thousands of other millworkers
whose memories were never written down

Preston was no ordinary town during the nineteenth century. While king cotton reigned supreme throughout Lancashire, the underlying ills associated with this industry were very often highlighted particularly starkly there. Child labour, shocking working conditions with appallingly long hours and pitifully low wages, as well as the constant risk of suffering horrific accidents in the cotton mills, all fostered a deep sense of hostility among the operatives towards the employers. Overcrowded and insanitary housing, disease, poverty and awful wretchedness were often to be witnessed in the fast-growing working-class districts of Preston. Against this backdrop the nascent trade unions and political and social reformers began to challenge the unbridled mastery of the millowners. Trade disputes, confrontations, lockouts, strikes and tragic episodes of violence were the inevitable consequence of this lethal mix of hardship and employer intransigence, and dominated affairs in the town for many years.

Acknowledgements

I would like to thank the staff at Lancashire Record Office in Bow Lane, Preston, along with their colleagues at the Harris Reference Library for the assistance they provided during the research for this book.

I would also like to thank Kevin and Tina Saint, along with my daughter Sarah Leigh for their invaluable help with the typing of the original manuscript.

Last, but certainly not least, I would like to thank my wife Gess, whose encouragement was greatly appreciated throughout my research and writing.

Introduction

THE STRUGGLES AND SUFFERINGS of the Preston cotton workers during the nineteenth century became famous well beyond the town itself, for during this turbulent period events occurred here which attracted the interest of the national media as well as being the cause of deep concern, distress and sometimes destitution for local people. The attention of the wealthy leaders of society and the impoverished workers alike was focused on Preston from all over Britain. In this period Preston differed little from many other industrial towns, as far as poor housing or unsatisfactory working conditions were concerned, but what set it apart from other places was the persistence of confrontation, and the numerous bitter disputes between the millmasters and their employees. This, together with continuous agitation for political and social reform, meant that Preston was often used as a barometer of change. Violent strikes, lockouts, and trade disputes ravaged the cotton industry and Preston secured an unwanted national notoriety.

These events happened a century and a half ago, and not only the participants but also the Preston cotton industry itself have disappeared. Only the history remains, but the city of Preston, as it has recently become, is now a vastly different place from the one that expanded so rapidly during the nineteenth century. New industries have replaced cotton, while the sprawling terraced communities of Avenham, North Road, Moor Lane, Lancaster Road and Maudland have largely been swept away. New generations of Prestonians have little or no knowledge of the cotton industry, and how powerful and dominant it was in their town. But it is to be hoped that, together with outsiders attracted here by the new city status and vibrant economy, they will read this story and then appreciate the trials and tribulations endured by the ordinary citizens of this area. The sacrifice and toil of the nineteenth-century workers laid the foundations for and helped to create great wealth, though it was not evenly shared. The Preston cotton operatives were hardy people, and were among the pioneers who enabled the industrial revolution to take root, thrive and develop throughout Britain as well as the western world. This book attempts to preserve the memory of their self-sacrifice and lifetimes of hardship, lives which often hovered on the brink of starvation. I sincerely hope that anyone who calls himself or herself a Prestonian remembers their struggles. Indeed, I hope that everyone remembers.

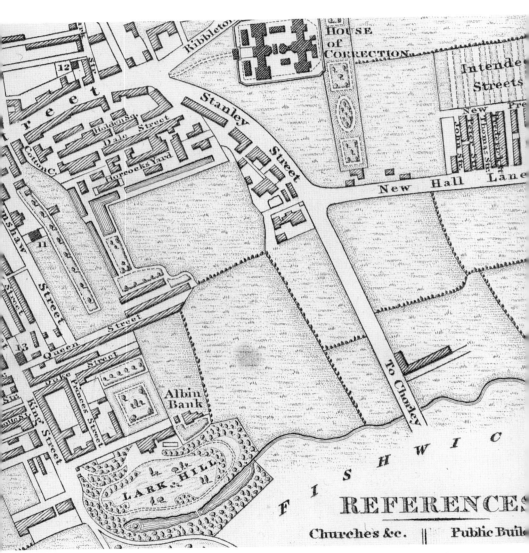

A detail of Baines' map of Preston, dating from 1824. Parts of the relatively affluent town can be seen around Lark Hill, while, top right, can be seen some of the new industrial housing around 'New Preston' on New Hall Lane.

CHAPTER ONE

The early years

D URING the Middle Ages, the small market town of Preston began to develop a small textile manufacturing trade, especially in wool and linen. Flax and hemp, for the manufacture of linen and canvas respectively, were grown locally, while wool was obtained from sheep which grazed on the fells and hillsides behind the town. Preston's geographical position in central Lancashire, on the old roadway to Lancaster in the north and Manchester or Warrington to the south, gave it an importance as a market town, and this, together with its administrative role and its legal and commercial business, enabled the community to thrive. Production of textiles was carried out by hand. Spinning the wool, flax or hemp fibres on a hand wheel was largely, but not always, a rural craft, while handloom weaving, whereby the spun yarn was made into cloth, was carried out extensively in rural or town areas. Until the middle of the eighteenth century, the woollen and worsted trade, after agriculture, was by far the most important manufacturing trade nationally. Cotton manufacturing was until that time a minor element, in Preston as elsewhere, though in some parts of Lancashire it was assuming a greater importance by the 1750s. The production of woollen goods continued virtually unchanged for generations: flocks of sheep were raised primarily for their wool rather than their meat by large landowners and smallholders alike. The wool was sold on to merchants or middlemen, who in turn passed it on to individuals, mainly of the labouring classes, who would spin it into yarn on the traditional hand spinning wheel. The people employed to spin this yarn were mainly women, children, elderly relatives or poor agricultural workers, who used this work to supplement an already meagre income.

Much of this work was contracted on a piece rate system, so in theory the quicker the job was completed, the faster it could be handed back to the contractor and the more wages could be earned. The spun yarn would then be contracted to handloom weavers to be woven into good quality cloth, again on a piece rate system. After bleaching or dyeing and finishing, the cloth was sent to the clothier to be tailored. The whole manufacturing process was

Preston and district in the early eighteenth century: a section of Morden's map of Lancashire. Preston was an ancient market town which came to be located at the centre of an extensive region of handloom weaving: in some townships a majority of households took part in the trade to some degree.

performed by hand, without artificial power, under the cottage or domestic system. Hand spinning on a wheel was regarded as unskilled work, even though considerable dexterity was required, but handloom weaving was seen as a skilled occupation. A good weaver could hold his head high in the local community. All in all, life for handloom weavers and their families from the mid-eighteenth century in the Preston area was, despite the inevitable fluctuations in trade, not uncomfortable. Weavers could earn good money and because of this many families engaged in agricultural work began to diversify, supplementing their family income with the earnings from weaving. Weavers had a reputation as extremely proud people with an air of independence – not least, they could work their own hours depending on motivation, a freedom envied by the labourers who worked the land from dawn to dusk for small remuneration.

The golden age for handloom weaving was the late eighteenth and early nineteenth centuries. The invention in 1733 of the flying shuttle, by John Kay of Bury, allowed the handloom weavers to produce finished cloth more quickly. The flying shuttle was widely adopted, and the increased output of cloth which this made possible placed heavy demands upon the spinners, who had to supply much more yarn. Delays or shortfalls in the output of yarn prevented the weaving end of the process from reaching its potential. The merchants and clothiers attempted to find a solution to this problem, just as the demand for cotton goods began to expand as population grew and the need for cheap fabrics increased exponentially. A series of inventions and improvements transformed the industry and, in consequence, changed Lancashire and Preston for ever. In the 1760s a Prestonian, Richard Arkwright, who was acutely aware of the inadequacies of hand spinning and probably aware of the riches to be made by advancing the whole process, began to study the idea of applying mechanical power to cotton spinning. After working secretly at night at the building at the bottom of Stoneygate now named after him, Arkwright House, in 1768 he applied for a patent for his new invention, the spinning or water frame. This invention, once perfected, allowed a major increase in the output of yarn. In 1770 James Hargreaves, a handloom weaver from Oswaldtwistle in Lancashire,

Richard Arkwright's water frame, one of the key technical advances in the development of the Lancashire cotton industry.
CARNEGIE COLLECTION

Arkwright House survives amid post-industrial dereliction at the bottom of Stoneygate largely thanks to a rescue campaign in the 1970s when it was converted to educational use. Arkwright worked in a room at the back of the house.

PHOTOGRAPH: CARNEGIE

patented his spinning jenny which, although quite different from Arkwright's frame, achieved the same results. With the availability of these machines the emergence of the factory system accelerated. Both machines were primarily powered by water, so the early entrepreneurs generally constructed the new factories in rural locations, or on the edges of towns, where there were fast-flowing rivers or streams.

The first cotton mill to be erected in Preston was in Moor Lane, on the site now occupied by the British Telecom building, in 1777. It was operated by a partnership of two men, Collinson and Watson, and initially, in the absence of a suitable stream, was driven by a combination of horse and wind power. This spinning mill did not last very long, but elsewhere in Lancashire many new ventures opened over the next 25 years. In 1779 Samuel Crompton of Bolton discovered that by combining the best principles of Arkwright's spinning frame and Hargreaves' spinning jenny, a much better machine could be constructed which would spin large quantities of very good, fine yarn. By simply winding a carriage inwards and outwards continuously, dozens of

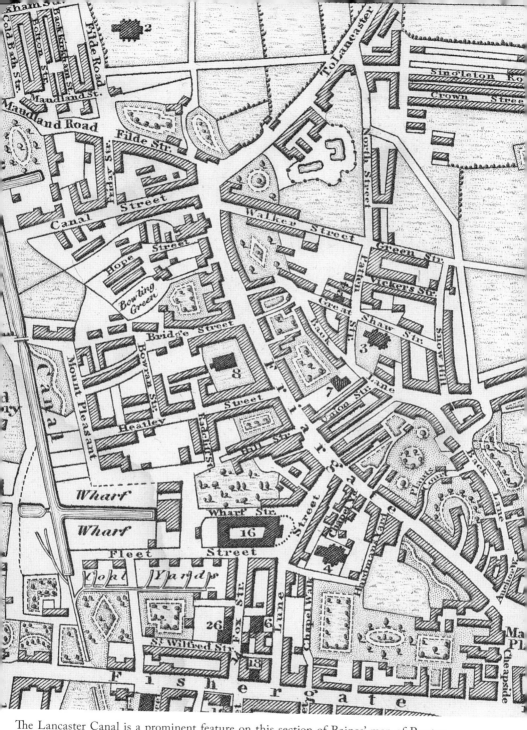

The Lancaster Canal is a prominent feature on this section of Baines' map of Preston, 1824. Kirkham Street is top left; Mount Pleasant is centre left; Moor Lane is top right, with rows of early terraced housing nearby.

Horrocks's Yellow Factory, with its 1791 datestone prominent on the façade. The cotton industry always provided work for large numbers of women as well as for men, and this group leaving the factory is made up mainly of women. The factory was demolished in 1942.

CARNEGIE COLLECTION

separate spindles could be activated. Crompton's discovery, because it was a mixture of the two previous inventions, was given the nickname 'mule'. Shortly afterwards, in 1781, James Watt worked out how to harness steam power to drive a rotary motion drive. This brilliant innovation could supply power to the new machines far more effectively. Steam power was not new – it had been used in colliery pumping engines in Lancashire since the early eighteenth century – but until this time was not used in a factory context.

First mechanisation, and then the adoption of steam power, made cotton-spinning highly efficient, and dramatically increased the output of yarn, so that the handloom weavers had almost unlimited potential for work. There was yarn in abundance, but the weaving stage of the process of cloth production was barely mechanised and was still almost totally dependent on human power. Although a powerloom for weaving cloth was patented in 1785 by the Reverend Edmund Cartwright, this machine was highly experimental, unreliable and had numerous technical defects. Handloom weaving remained safe for another three decades, during which the weavers enjoyed unparalleled prosperity and high status within the growing industrial community. Meanwhile, Preston's cotton industry continued to grow. The man responsible for the introduction of large-scale cotton manufacturing in Preston was John Horrocks. Born in 1768 at Edgworth near Bolton, as a young man he appreciated the potential of these new inventions, acquired a spinning frame of his own, and began to produce yarn. He then sold this yarn to John Watson, one of the partners in the doomed Moor Lane enterprise opened in 1777. Supposedly after a quarrel with Watson over a commercial arrangement, Horrocks moved to Preston, setting up a small carding and spinning business in Turks Head Yard, off Church Street. It was far more successful than the businesses of his erstwhile associate. In 1791, when he was still only 23, John Horrocks erected the famous Yellow Factory, near the junction of Church Street and Stanley Street. From these small beginnings would grow one of the world's great cotton firms, carrying the name of Horrocks, and of Preston, around the globe, and remaining a key player in the cotton trade for over 150 years. For some, there was a lot of money to be made in cotton: Richard Arkwright, the famous Prestonian who had by now been knighted, died aged 60 in 1792, leaving an estate valued at over £500,000 (perhaps £100 million in modern terms). By 1799, John Horrocks and his brother Samuel had built five more spinning mills in various locations in Preston.

These processes of change in the textile industry had a profound effect upon working people and upon the movement of population. The creation of the factory system altered the demand for labour, requiring large numbers in

The archetypal cotton mill dating from the apogee of the Lancashire industry:
Horrocks's Centenary Mill of 1912 on New Hall Lane was located near the original
centre of the Horrocks empire.
PHOTOGRAPH: CARNEGIE

one place, and so drew people from the countryside to the fast-growing towns. There was plenty of employment in the newly constructed mills such as those owned by Horrocks in Preston. But there was a serious downside. The factory system meant that the individual worker was depersonalised, losing identity and losing control over his or her life. A strict routine of very long working hours had to be endured daily; lateness or absence, even in times of sickness, were not tolerated; and the mill's timetable dominated the worker's existence. Discipline was extremely harsh, with automatic fines for faulty work, the slightest misdemeanour severely punished, and behaviour during work hours, such as talking and resting, rigorously regulated. The child workers could expect beatings from time to time, either from the overlooker, who would supervise their work, or from ordinary millhands in their team.

The population of Preston had grown steadily during the second half of the eighteenth century, to reach some 6,000 by 1780, but thereafter its growth accelerated and by 1802, when the Horrocks brothers opened their fifth mill, it had reached 12,000. The majority of the newcomers had little choice about where they lived – they sought accommodation wherever they could. Often this meant cramming into the tiny dwellings that either already existed in the narrow passages, courtyards and alleyways of the town centre, or newly built hovels, hastily constructed in the same confined locations off Church Street or Churchgate, Fishergate and Friargate. In these cramped, overcrowded conditions, with primitive sanitation and rapidly increasing squalor, virtually no provision for refuse disposal, many of the newcomers must have yearned for the country areas from which they came. As the cotton industry expanded further, and the number of workers and thus of residents continued to grow rapidly, further housing development shifted to the edge of the old town, as near as possible to the new mills but on greenfield sites. Among the earliest new housing areas, built over with small terraced housing, were Fylde Road and Kirkham Street, parts of Avenham, the east side of New Hall Lane, and the area close to Marsh Lane. In some parts, though, a very distinctive form of housing, specially designed for handloom weaving, was provided. This was a transitional period in our industrial development, because cotton spinning had been mechanised but weaving was still dependent on human power. With this in mind, many early terraced dwellings in Preston, built close to the spinning mills, were constructed with a substantial cellar or loom shop. This meant that the finished spun yarn could be 'put out' to nearby hand weavers to be made into cloth. Although attempts to mechanise weaving and integrate this process in to the factories were regularly made, not until the 1820s did steam-powered weaving become both technologically and financially viable, and it would be many years before handloom weaving was completely superseded in mid-Lancashire.

In 1804, with the cotton industry firmly established in Preston, its founding father, John Horrocks, died suddenly, aged 36. His death came at a time of great acceleration in the industry, with other entrepreneurs appearing on the scene. For example, John Paley and his partner Richard Riley had opened a mill close to Heatley Street. Most of the new industrialists had previously had connections with John Horrocks, and no doubt, were directly or indirectly indebted to him. Preston continued to grow at an unprecedented rate throughout this early phase, despite the commercial, economic, social and political difficulties which were encountered throughout Britain during the Napoleonic Wars. Among the most immediate of all the problems and hardships faced by ordinary people was the rapid price rise in wheat and other grains, leading inevitably to the high cost of bread. By 1808, severe economic distress was affecting many parts of Britain and strong political action was applied to stifle the emergence of workers' organisations, which were held by those in authority to be subversive and likely to foment further discontent.

The Combination Acts of 1799/1800 forbade the 'combining' of two or more persons for the purpose of obtaining an increase in wages, or agitating for better working conditions. This legislation created a great deal of bitterness, but it remained in force for 24 long years. Nevertheless, in 1808 men and women of the Preston handloom weaving community resorted to protest and agitated for higher wages in the face of increasing hardship. The weavers, many of whom were proud to be following in the trade of their fathers and grandfathers, demonstrated in large numbers with the hope of influencing debate on their plight. Little is known of the infrastructure of this early organisation in Preston. The Combination Acts imposed savage penalties for this early form of trade union activity, so maintaining secrecy was extremely important. Paid spies and informers were known to infiltrate such organisations, and therefore written minutes or statements were hardly ever maintained for fear of prosecution. The later local historian and journalist Anthony Hewitson stated that in 1808

> there was a demand for higher wages by hand loom weavers. Some of these men were employed indirectly by Samuel Horrocks to the east of the town in New Hall Lane fields in specially built hand loom sheds, or houses for these weavers nearby, to which he outsourced work. On 2 June, a state of tension existed in the town as groups of weavers assembled. Some time approaching midday these groups were dispersed. The following day, even larger groups assembled. The authorities, fearing machine breaking order the military to be on full alert and arms were distributed. However, the weavers realised the futility of engaging the military and the 84th regiment and dispersed. About 20 per cent of Preston inhabitants were in severe distress. A fund was set up and the poor were relieved twice a week.

A contemporary historian, Peter Whittle, also briefly described events: 'In February 1808, 1,000 poor families were relieved by donations from fund. The corporation donated £120 on top of this.'

It is clear that a substantial proportion of the inhabitants of Preston were in a state of severe poverty during 1808 and, as Hewitson implied, the handloom weavers appeared to suffer most. By this time, although handloom weaving was experiencing perhaps its greatest levels of output and employment, wage levels had started to fall. This apparent contradiction is easily explained – too many people had taken up handloom weaving in the previous twenty years, so there was now an oversupply of labour and thus individual wages fell. However, a more serious threat was beginning to appear. As we have seen, Edmund Cartwright developed the first powered loom in 1785, and in 1804 William Radcliffe of Stockport improved the efficiency of the machine. A few Lancashire millowners acquired these machines, from about 1806 onwards. As populations, and the number of handloom weavers, grew, there was a danger that inexperienced weavers would take up the trade and that quality would fall. The apprenticeship system, such as it was, disappeared, and the trade was completely unregulated. Millowners could force down wages, because there were simply too many weavers for any workers to insist on a realistic wage.

With the industry now destabilised, weavers had to toil for very long hours to produce sufficient finished cloth and earn an increasingly meagre income. In May 1808, with the old structure of the trade facing complete collapse, a petition – reputedly signed by over 130,000 weavers, and calling for a legal minimum wage – was presented to Parliament. This was no ordinary cry for help by a group of workers, for it was also supported by the more humane employers, who saw it as a means of enforcing fairer conditions of competition on their less scrupulous rivals. Parliament, predictably enough, rejected the petition out of hand, leaving the industry at the continuing mercy of market forces. No widespread rioting was reported among Preston's weaving community, who now seemed resigned to their fate. On the other hand some 15,000 Manchester weavers embarked on strike action and took to the streets. The magistrates ordered the dispersal of the mobs, which ultimately ended in violence. Battle lines were being drawn between capital and labour, and there is some evidence to suggest that Preston handloom weavers maintained a shadowy form of organisation during the following years, campaigning for a minimum wage and parliamentary reform. Similar movements existed in Stockport, Ashton-under-Lyne, Saddleworth, Oldham, Lancaster, Eccles and elsewhere in Lancashire, with Manchester the hub of this movement. For the time being, the Preston weavers appeared to have accepted that this particular struggle against the employers was lost. What battles would their children and grandchildren have to fight?

CHAPTER TWO

The quest for reform

A MONG the new generation of factory workers, the cotton mule spinners emerged as the most radical. In 1810, although trade unionism still illegal, Preston mule spinners, in co-operation with a secret union organisation based in Manchester, took the dangerous decision to strike. How many spinners embarked on this action is unclear, but the aim of these men was to raise wage rates in Preston to the levels paid in Manchester. This same issue dominated industrial relations for many years to come and was a constant source of tension between Preston millowners and their employees. The tactic of the spinners involved encouraging a series of selective town strikes, supported by contributions from mule spinners in cotton towns across Lancashire. Running considerable risks, a body of delegates from different towns coordinated the dispute, raising over £122 for the Preston spinners. Nevertheless, although the Preston men stayed out for over two months, the strike eventually collapsed, and the men were forced to return to work on the employers' terms. The Preston spinners were defeated, but it was clear that some among them had the courage and motivation to fight for increased wages and better conditions. In 1811 and 1812 there were the episodes of machine-breaking, by handloom operatives, which history records as 'Luddism'. This movement began in Nottinghamshire, when desperately poor framework knitters embarked on a wave of violence, provoked by employers who sought to flood the market with shoddy goods produced on new wide frames. The Nottinghamshire stockingers formed a secret organisation, under the alleged leadership of one Ned Ludd. The Luddites knew full well that a conviction for machine breaking meant transportation or even execution, but they continued to meet, and agitate. It is unclear whether Ned Ludd was a real person, but the name passed into legend. Luddism spread to Cheshire, Yorkshire and Lancashire, where there were comparable waves of machine breaking, this time directed at the early versions of power looms. There is no evidence of machine-smashing at Preston, but at Westhoughton near Bolton a cotton mill and its powerlooms were destroyed, for which several alleged rioters, including a boy of 12, were executed.

The government was still terrified that the revolutionary ideas from France would be brought to Britain and take root, and that working-class radicalism would destabilise the nation. It therefore continued to emphasise the illegality of combinations, forcing workers to unite in secret. Members faced the constant threat of arrest, so it was essential to initiate new members by administering a secret oath. The pledging of such an oath was not to be done lightly, its essential point being the promise, very often unto death, never to divulge the names of other members in the event of arrest or interrogation. To counter these dangerous elements of solidarity, the authorities began to recruit a network of spies and informers from among working people, in order to infiltrate the unions and associations. Agents provocateur would urge moderate unionists to commit acts of violence, while judges, sometimes unable to convict for offences under the Combination Acts, could instead punish, using the evidence of informers, under the Illegal Oaths Act. Harsh sentences, including transportation to the colonies, could be handed out under this legislation. Many people ended their lives in penal servitude thousands of miles away, forever separated from family and friends.

By 1818, some 27 years after John Horrocks had come to Preston, this had become firmly established as a cotton town. A whole generation was accustomed to the hardships of working in the spinning mills. But to add to their difficulties was the impact of widespread national economic problems, and the associated political and social turbulence. Although Britain had emerged victorious at Waterloo, the financial consequences of 22 years of more or less continuous war were ruinous. The national debt had increased considerably and although a short-lived boom prevailed after Waterloo, by 1818 the inevitable slump had caused unemployment to rise alarmingly, bringing much distress to a substantial portion of the population. The restrictions on wheat imports, initiated by Parliament under the Corn Laws in order to protect landowners and farmers, created further increases in bread prices. The 1818 recession was accompanied by rounds of wage-cutting and the weavers, now vulnerable to mechanisation, were particularly at risk. Towards the end of September 1818 a group of perhaps 1200 weavers paraded through the streets of Preston demanding higher wages. The day after this gesture of open defiance, another large body of weavers assembled at the top of High Street (near the present Ringway). After some discussion, they agreed to march in a mock funeral procession towards Gallows Hill on Garstang Road (where the English Martyrs Church stands today). There, a spokesman delivered a solemn oration and, after the digging of a mock grave, a set of weaver's tools was buried. A different 'ceremony' had taken place the previous week, when the name of Horrocks & Co. had been drawn from a green bag and notice given that the weavers would not work for this employer. Yet again, though, no benefits were derived from these demonstrations.

Low and uncertain wages were not the only issue. Working conditions were deteriorating, with a 75-hour working week for adults commonplace, and children as young as ten enduring a 60-hour week. The sufferings of ordinary folk were obvious to anyone who cared to look, and radical and liberal thinkers and politicians of all classes seriously questioned many aspects of the industrial economy, debating such issues as profits in relation to wages, factory legislation, and employee rights. A local weekly newssheet, the *Preston Chronicle*, was the focus of much of this opinion via its news columns and letters to the editor. Much concern was centred on the controversial issue of child employment within the cotton mills, and especially the number of hours that children should labour each week. In February 1818 the *Chronicle* reported on a parliamentary debate about child labour in the Lancashire cotton manufactories. Sir Robert Peel the elder was campaigning for a substantial reduction in the working hours of children, and had held aloft a petition signed by 6,000 young cotton workers employed in the Manchester area. He informed the House that he had unexpectedly been approached by a number of them who knew that a reduction in working hours would be accompanied by a reduction in wages, but

> These people, who had perhaps done more for their Country, in point of labour, than any other class of individuals, were willing to submit to any privation rather than continue to be oppressed by excessive labour. They were made to work in badly ventilated and overheated rooms not less than fourteen or fifteen hours each day and they could not endure such confinement. However, there was a period when that excessive labour proved to oppressive to be supported by the human constitution ... when so much was done to increase the prosperity of our trade, then surely, the House should not shrink from extending its protection to those by whom the manufactures that fed that trade, were carried on.

He proposed that the labour of these children 'may be confined to Ten hours per day, allowing them a half hour for breakfast and one hour for dinner'.

Many opponents of reform argued that no employer forced these children into employment and parents should be free to do as they pleased with their own offspring. The reformers countered this by claiming that the wages of adults were so meagre that most families had little choice but to send children to work – and that so long as there was a ready supply of child workers, adult wages would remain low. The opponents of child labour pushed their case strongly, and the intellectuals and clandestine trade unionists of Preston carried on the debate locally. A week after Peel's speech and petition in the House, a letter from an ordinary cotton worker appeared in the *Chronicle*. The worker accepted that it might be thought he was exaggerating his case, but

> I am one of the number of those employed in cotton factories and have been so from my early years, so that consequently, it must be allowed that I know the ill effects which such long confinement, day after day, has upon my own health and which cannot fail to have on others. To proceed to my subject, it is a notorious fact that there are a number of children sent to the factories at the early age of six years, where they are confined from six o' clock in the morning till a quarter or half after eight at night, with the solitary allowance of from thirty or forty minutes during dinner, the rest of their meals they have to eat as well as they can and work during the same time. This is a barbarous piece of inhumanity, that they should not be allowed proper time to take their meat and which often gets covered with fluke and dirt which is generally flying about in such places.

The writer then raised the question of education, pointing out that

> After being immured in a hot factory fourteen hours in the day, there is but little, very little time left, either for education or recreation. No wonder then, that so few of them have any education when they have not sufficient time allowed them to obtain it. I thank God I was kept at school till I was nine years old before I was sent to the factory, as in that time, I learned to read and write tolerably well and by acquiring a little improvement since, as well as I could, I have been able to give you the present sketch ... I appeal to all those endowed with the feelings of humanity, if it is not high time that some provision should be made against this increasing evil, which loudly calls for investigation and which has been the cause of snatching a many children off, at an early age, who might have become useful members of society. Yet should they have the good fortune to arrive at the years of manhood, like the tender bud, nipped in its infancy by the chilling blast, they may drag out a few years of miserable existence, but will seldom fail to meet with a premature grave.

Despite strong organised resistance to Peel's bill, in 1819 the Factory Act became law, but a compromise with the vested interests in the cotton industry meant that it only outlawed the employment of free children under nine years of age in cotton mills, and restricted the working hours for children aged between nine and sixteen in the same industry to twelve hours a day. For many reformers this limited Act was little better than a defeat, for a 60–70 hour week for children aged nine and over was still perfectly legal. The 1819 Act made no provision for paid factory inspectors – so who was to check

The republican Richard Carlile commissioned this print showing his representation of the events at 'Peterloo'.

its application? – and the restrictions did not apply to orphaned or pauper children. Realistically, the Act could never be enforced and unscrupulous employers blatantly ignored it. Orphaned children could still be farmed out to employers under the notion of an apprenticeship, as could pauper children whose parents could no longer support them. Some of these unfortunate children found themselves under compassionate employers, who gave them some education and treated them well, but many others were put out to work with brutal employers under appalling conditions. Death, or terrible deformities caused by poor diet, restricted bone development and excessive working hours at such a young age, could be the result. Some ran away from this shocking existence, to become street children and survive by scavenging, begging or stealing. The option of enlisting in the army or navy was available to some boys, but girls who absconded might find only menial service, or sexual exploitation and prostitution.

Joseph Livesey, the well-known temperance advocate and writer, was born at Walton-le-Dale in 1794. As a child, he often saw pauper apprentices from the Penwortham factory attending church on Sundays. Many years later, he remembered them as

Poor, squalid, deformed beings, the most pitiful objects I think I have ever beheld. They were apprenticed to a system to which nothing but West Indian slavery can bear any analogy. Many of the children were obtained from the Foundling Hospital in London and were crooked legged through having to stop the machinery by placing their knees frequently against it.

Britain had started the abolition of the slave trade in 1807, yet allowed the employment of 'unfree' children in its industries for many years to come.

The opening of the door to very modest reform prompted a wave of further agitation. On 16 August 1819 a huge demonstration was held in Manchester in support of democratic reform. Over 60,000 people assembled in St Peter's Field to hear the well-known Radical, Henry 'Orator' Hunt. As this vast crowd awaited the speeches, local magistrates decided to arrest Hunt who, apparently, was willing to give himself up to the authorities rather than provoke a potentially dangerous situation. But the magistrates ordered the Manchester Yeomanry to charge the crowd, with sabres drawn. The militia rode in as instructed, causing panic and extensive bloodshed – eleven of the crowd were killed and many hundreds badly wounded. The 'Peterloo Massacre', as it was called in mock reference to Waterloo, was a political watershed. The Yeomanry and magistrates evaded or avoided blame, and the government, convinced that national insurrection was imminent, passed legislation which gave local magistrates the power of rapid summary conviction of political offenders, the right to search private or public houses, the ability to declare as illegal any meetings of which they did not approve, and the right to ban any publications to which they considered as seditious or blasphemous, while at national level a heavy tax was imposed on radical newspapers and journals. But, rather than stifling radical opinion, these measures in fact had the opposite effect. Liberal attitudes hardened, while the editors, publishers, printers and vendors of radical publications submitted to prison sentences rather than accept the principle of the legislation. In Manchester, as in the adjacent towns such as Stockport, Ashton-under-Lyne and Oldham which had long been influenced by the Manchester operatives, the tragedy of Peterloo gave a greater momentum to trade unionism.

These houses on Mount Pleasant Street West were built right at the end of the eighteenth century in the first phase of industrial development. In this 1952 photograph one can just make out two dogs, a little girl playing by the roadside and, on the far right, a young boy. It was on Mount Pleasant that Andrew Ryding lived at the time when he attacked Samuel Horrocks in 1822.

When industrialisation came to Preston the town was a relatively compact county town, and most of the early workers' housing was built fairly close to the old town centre. Because land values increased greatly in this area as the town grew, and because most of the early houses were cramped and of poor quality, very few indeed survived redevelopment and slum clearance. This pair of early workers' houses are on Marsh Lane, near its junction with Friargate. Perhaps they survived because they happened to be located between commercial properties?

PHOTOGRAPH: CARNEGIE, 2007

The Manchester operatives were willing to agitate publicly for higher wages and democratic reform, but those in Preston were far fewer in number and could not muster mass demonstrations on a Mancunian scale. Neither were they as well organised. A few arrests of the leaders in their ranks would have shattered such a small movement. Although by 1819 the Preston cotton spinners had a trade union with an elected committee, it had failed to attract a substantial membership among the millworkers. Among those on the committee of the Preston spinners' union in 1819 was a young man called Andrew Ryding. He was 18 years old, lived in Mount Pleasant (near Marsh Lane) and was employed as a spinner at James Kay's cotton mill. He was also a committed trade unionist. In 1819 James Kay and some other Preston cotton employers decided to reduce wages, on the pretext of bad trading conditions. This immediately provoked a six-week strike among the spinning operatives, who were eventually forced to return to work on the employers' terms. Whether James Kay knew of Ryding's involvement with the clandestine spinners committee is unclear, but several weeks later he confronted the employee and accused him of producing faulty thread. Ryding maintained that the thread shown to him was not his work, pointing out that from its appearance it must have been produced on two different machines. Kay did not believe him, and sacked him. Unable to find work anywhere in Preston, possibly as a result of 'blacklisting', Ryding left to seek employment in Manchester, where he subsequently wrote an anonymous letter to Samuel Horrocks, the prominent Preston mill owner:

> Sir, if you do not advance the wages of cotton spinners at least twenty per cent, you may expect your life to be taken by a cotton spinner of Manchester. You were the cause of the falling of wages in Preston. There are many cotton masters deserving to lose there lives, but you are, it is said, and I believe it is true, the worst of them all.

Ryding returned to Preston sometime in 1822, to learn that three of his friends, named Naylor, Hodgson and Holland, had been arrested for belonging to a trade union. He himself could not secure work anywhere in the town and was supported by his impoverished parents. On the morning of 27 July, after getting up in the morning, Ryding concealed a kitchen cleaver under his coat and went to the parish church. As the congregation left after the service

High Street, looking east, *c.*1960. Now the site of the ring road, it was here in 1818 that hundreds of disgruntled handloom weavers assembled to demand higher wages.

he spotted Samuel Horrocks and followed him along Church Street, before striking him twice with the cleaver on the back of the head and shouting 'I will kill you'. He then threw down the cleaver, ran a short distance, but was apprehended and sent to Lancaster castle to await trial. In court, a witness, Anne Johnson, said that after the attack she saw Ryding run away but stop of his own accord and say, 'Take me, Take me'. Ryding's parents gave evidence, telling the court that when he was in one of his strange moods, they were frightened of being attacked. Elizabeth, his mother, added that on the fateful morning her son had put on two shirts, two pair of stockings and even cleaned his boots twice. Her own brother, she said, had died of a fever, raving like a madman, and Andrew was very often like his uncle.

Ryding himself made no attempt to deny the attack, but instead sought to explain the reason for the vicious assault. It was, he said, to draw attention to the differences that existed between the masters and the men. If he had simply hit Horrocks with his fists, he would have been tried by the Preston magistrates who were, he claimed, all friends of Horrocks. Being a poor man, he would be denied justice. So he decided to attempt to murder Horrocks, without actually wanting to kill him (hence the use of a blunt cleaver, to cut and bruise but not actually kill). He realised that he might be hanged, but had decided to go ahead anyway because in the court at Lancaster he could tell people of the injustices whereby the government allowed the masters to combine to reduce wages, but stopped working men from combining to protect wages.

After the judge's summing up the jury retired and in only a few minutes returned with a verdict of not guilty on the grounds of insanity. Passing sentence, Judge Bayley declared that because Ryding was insane and a danger to other people, he could not go free and ordered that he should be incarcerated in Lancaster Gaol for the rest of his life. After the trial, a great deal of information concerning Andrews' background came to light. At the age of six or seven, he had been sent to work as a piecer in one of the Horrocks mills. His father, Thomas, had served in the Royal Navy during the Napoleonic wars and had lost a leg in battle, but after his discharge worked as best he could as a bandage maker, while sometimes performing inoculations. Since the age of twelve, Andrew suffered from severe headaches, often accompanied with a ringing sensation in the ears, and some years later had contracted a fever which resulted in violent head pain and a slight discharge from the ears. He began to experience some deafness and sought help from the Preston dispensary, but his medicine proved to be ineffective. Sometimes the pain became so bad that he did not realise what he was doing. Nothing more was ever heard of Andrew Ryding.

CHAPTER THREE

Combination and radicalism

DESPITE the Andrew Ryding affair, the infant Preston spinners' union carried on illegally – when meeting in public it adopted the guise of a friendly society to avoid prosecution. In his *History of Preston* Hewitson describes this period:

> The operative cotton spinners in 1823 held Society meetings in the Green Man public house in Lord Street. The local authorities, quick to stamp their authority and prevent possible agitation, which could damage Preston's emerging economy, became uneasy at these supposed meetings. On one occasion, Police raided the pub causing the participants to flee or hide nearby and books were seized. However no evidence of conspiracy was discovered. Constant surveillance was kept upon any suspicious meetings, with Police regularly in attendance, ensuring no illegal oaths were taken or subversive language, or ideas mooted.

In 1824 the Combination Acts were finally repealed, so workers were free to join together without fear of prosecution. A year later, though, that right was again restricted, to matters of wages and hours of labour only. Any attempt to obstruct or molest non-union workers was strictly forbidden, as was any union influence over the proportion of apprentices to skilled people in the workplace. The 1824 legislation did represent progress, but victimisation by employers against union activists continued, and the 1797 Illegal Oaths Act remained on the statute books. From time to time it was still employed against trade unionists. Another contentious issue was the theft or misappropriation of union funds by corrupt officials. Trade unions had no legal right to sue in such circumstances, even if theft was irrefutably proved. Despite this new legal right to combine, life for the Preston cotton operatives carried on much the same, with a continuing struggle to achieve fair wages and acceptable working conditions. Small gains were hard won and even more jealously guarded. The only legislation that could really assist in 1824 would have been a guarantee of a legal minimum wage, or some other form of financial assistance, both of which were rejected out of hand.

Then in 1826, following a speculative boom in the cotton trade, there was a tremendous slump associated with the near collapse of the banking industry. Manufacturers faced serious reductions in profits and the unfortunate handloom weaver, at the bottom of the hierarchy in the industry, bore the brunt of this depression. Wages per cut of finished cloth were drastically reduced throughout Lancashire's handloom weaving communities, resulting in near starvation and total despair. Many people could take no more and in April, in East Lancashire, there was extensive rioting. For nearly a week, desperate groups of handloom weavers and their supporters vented their anger towards what they regarded as the source of their plight – the factories. Though they realised that the process of technological advance could not be reversed, in their frustration the weavers attacked the powerlooms, smashing every one to which they could gain access. Episodes of loom-breaking occurred in and around Accrington, Oswaldtwistle, Blackburn, Darwen, Rawtenstall, and Chorley. In Chadderton six rioters were shot dead, among them a woman, as the military were mobilised to quell the disturbances, and dozens were arrested. In less than a week, over 1,000 power looms were destroyed.

In Preston there was no rioting or destruction, despite the considerable handloom weaving population, although the authorities began to apprehend known ringleaders and agitators. Such information must have been supplied by spies or informers within the weaving communities, or from the accounts of people present at the riots further east. On Wednesday 26 April 1826, in an early morning raid, a detachment of soldiers and special constables seized a man named Simeon Wright at Samlesbury. Wright, aged 26 and a weaver at Samlesbury mill, was transferred with others to the House of Correction at Preston. Fearful that an attempt might be made to free the prisoners, a group of armed cavalry escorted the party. In August 1826 sixty people, including twelve women, stood trial at Lancaster castle accused of various offences related to the April riots. Simeon Wright was charged with rioting at three factories in Blackburn and was labelled as a ringleader. He denied ever being at the scene of the violence, but was found guilty and, with forty others, was sentenced to death. There was, however, a recommendation for leniency, and all the death sentences were commuted. Of the 41 people who were originally sentenced to be executed, 31 received prison sentences ranging from three to eighteen months, while the other ten, who were considered the worst offenders, were transported for life to Australia. Simeon Wright from Samlesbury was among them. Never again would the handloom weaving

The little Roman Catholic church of St Mary behind Friargate lay quite close to the site of a much earlier religious building and catered for one of the town's principal Catholic communities until it was demolished in 1990. A statue with a plaque set within a small cubicle is all that remains of the church. The site is now a small car park. The earlier building on the site was the first official Catholic chapel in the town, in the early 1770s.

PHOTOGRAPH: CARNEGIE, 1988

communities engage in widespread violence in Lancashire and for many the only option was to abandon the trade and seek work elsewhere.

Despite the growing levels of overcrowding and the increasingly insanitary and unhealthy urban environment, newcomers continued to pour in to Preston. From a population of about 12,000 in 1801, by 1831 the town had grown to 33,000. Much of this exceptional increase was the result of continuing migration from the countryside, but a steady influx of Irish people was also coming to Preston. Many of the Irish immigrants sought employment in the cotton mills, but often encountered bitter hostility from the local population on racial grounds. Preston already had a large Catholic community, so religious sectarianism was not the main cause of the antagonism. Soon, an Irish ghetto emerged in Preston, centred on a cluster of streets and courts in the vicinity of the present Fylde Road roundabout and university buildings. There were many Irish elsewhere – for example, in the Manchester Road area

– but this was among the worst housing in the town. In 1831, the majority of the town's inhabitants still lived in the older Friargate, Fishergate and Avenham districts, but new housing, of deplorable quality, was expanding outwards from the town centre. The prospect of steady employment awaited those willing to work in the cotton mills, although the working conditions were harsh and dangerous. Safety legislation designed to protect millworkers was almost non-existent. William Dodd, in his book, *The Factory System Illustrated*, graphically describes human consequences of working conditions in the northern factories during this period:

Jonathon Oddson of Bolton Le Moors: His legs were deformed, his knees are both turned in, almost wrap over each other. In the act of walking he has to move the centre of gravity from side to side and balance himself like a ropedancer.

Jervis Hartley of Bradford: At seventeen he was completely done up. His limbs were so painful that he could scarcely get from home to work. He had no appetite for food. His eyes are damaged, as are his ears, his legs are miserably deformed and his right knee turns in and his left out. He says that he often wished he had been born a horse, a cow or a dog.

Joseph Lockett of Macclesfield: He worked in the mill until he was twenty, when he was done up. He is unable now to walk across the floor. He was so lame that he had to be carried to work and back. He sits in an armchair like an old man of ninety years of age though he is only twenty-four.

Bridget Lyons an Irish girl: At nineteen years of age she went to work as a piecer. After twenty weeks she met with an accident. She was in the act of picking up some cotton waste near an upright shaft, which was not sufficiently guarded. The shaft caught her clothes and wound her round it dashing her head against the wall and other obstructions. Being dreadfully crushed and bruised she was taken to the infirmary were she remained for thirty-eight weeks and had both legs amputated, the right above the knee and the left below the knee. She now has crutches and wooden leg.

Mary Jones, a Mother of several children: She worked near an upright shaft near which was the coupling boxes used for the coupling shaft. From the boxes projected a key. In passing the key one night, the key, which turned as the shaft turned, caught her clothes and dragged her round for several minutes. No one could find the engineer to stop the engine. The shaft was a short distance from the wall and her head and legs were dashed against the wall every time the shaft went round. The wall was covered with blood and hair. She was taken away a lifeless corpse.

William Hall of Preston: He went to work in a mill at Preston when seven years old. He wrote in 1826, I had to rise early and work late. My orders were never to sit down during the hours of actual work. I have been knocked down without warning and brutally kicked and dare not complain. Once I was fifteen minutes late for work and for this offence I was beaten, kicked and whipped until my whole body was covered in weals and bruises.

Since the early years of the industrial revolution, many educated people from all backgrounds, horrified by the conditions to which working folk were exposed, campaigned vigorously for social change. Known collectively as radicals, some fought passionately for parliamentary reform, with a view of a more democratic system for all, while others advocated a strong trade union movement. Several such idealists have a place in Preston's history. Among them was an Irishman, John Doherty, who started work in a textile mill in Ulster at the age of ten and settled in Manchester around 1816. An ardent follower of Robert Owen, whom many regard as the father of British socialism, Doherty was active in the underground Manchester cotton spinners' union, where his dedication and hard work soon earned him the position of secretary. His articles in radical newsprints, together with his organisational abilities, quickly brought him to the attention of the authorities.

Doherty's vision was to expand the spinners' union throughout Lancashire and beyond, and to pursue the goal of a general national union of all trades. This led to his conviction for conspiracy, and a sentence of two years' imprisonment in Lancaster castle in 1819. His efforts motivated many cotton operatives throughout Lancashire, including Preston, to maintain an organisation within each district and to forge links with other areas. Some regarded Doherty as a visionary, and he certainly inspired many inexperienced union organisations with the confidence to negotiate with the cotton masters. On 28 May 1831 he visited Preston, where he refrained from discussing trade union issues and instead addressed a gathering on the question of parliamentary reform, of which he was a passionate advocate. The campaign for reform had gained considerable support among all classes and a new Reform Bill was eagerly anticipated. Doherty spoke for over half an hour, and the Whit Monday holiday crowd listened attentively. Another radical destined to play a part in Preston's history was Henry Hunt. A gentleman farmer and brewer, he was in the forefront in the struggle for electoral reform. Known for his brilliant public speeches and firebrand nature, Hunt had already been imprisoned for his part in the Peterloo meeting in 1819, and he continued to campaign for universal manhood suffrage, the abolition of rotten boroughs, and the enfranchisement of the industrial towns and cities. He was a true friend of the working masses throughout his life. Hunt stood as a candidate for Preston in the 1830 election, against the powerful interests of the Stanley family and won the seat. In Preston, uniquely among English boroughs, most working men were entitled to vote, and in 1830 they demonstrated their power and independent spirit. The Stanley family, deeply shocked by this rebuff, immediately severed their ancient connections with the town.

Preston was now firmly on the map as a radical centre. Hunt and others campaigned vociferously for electoral reform and in October 1831 the Commons at last passed a Reform Bill. Its rejection in the House of Lords provoked serious widespread rioting in towns and cities throughout the land – Bristol, Nottingham, Derby and London all saw major destruction. Preston initially remained quiet, but then violence suddenly erupted in the town. On Monday 21 November 1831 people began to assemble about the town, in an apparent display of solidarity with workers in other towns. Hunt had been consulted the previous week when, at a meeting of the leading supporters of reform, it was agreed to present a series of resolutions to the mayor, and to arrange a meeting of the Preston operatives to discuss recent developments. After 9 a.m. some 40 individuals, mainly men and boys, gathered in Crown Street, with a banner bearing the inscription CROWN STREET DISTRICT NO 9 DEATH OR GLORY MY BOYS. They marched to Chadwick's Orchard, where a large crowd was assembling and being addressed by John Taylor, who urged the crowd to remain peaceful. As the meeting ended, about 100 men and youths broke away and headed towards Grundy's, the machine manufacturers of Tithebarn Street. There, an attempt was made to persuade the employees to turn out, but the gates were firmly closed and after a while the group moved on to Francis Sleddon's machine shop. There, with numbers increasing all the time, they turned out the workforce, some of who joined the agitators. Now heavily reinforced, the mob returned to Grundy's and, though kept at bay for well over an hour, they eventually battered down the factory gate. Once inside, some men extinguished the fire in the steam-engine boiler, bringing the factory machinery to a halt. Several constables had arrived at the scene, intent on arresting the principal ringleaders, but they had to stand aside after being surrounded and threatened. Even though Grundy's employees refused to join the rioters, a manager decided it was to dangerous to resume production, so money was made available for the hands to enjoy an afternoon of drinking in the Blackamoors public house on Lancaster Road.

The mob then went to Francis Sleddon's cotton mill at Hanover Street, off North Road, where they assaulted Sleddon and forced his employees out on the street. Lambert and Stephenson's Brunswick Place mill near Kent Street was the next target, but there the workers had anticipated trouble and fled, leaving the mill empty. As the protesters headed back towards the town centre, towards Ainsworth & Sons' factory in Church Street, they met no resistance. They stormed into the mill yard, successfully demanding that the operatives should cease work, but did no damage. At the mill of Horrocks, Miller & Co. in Stanley Street the employees were on their dinner break, so Riley's premises in London Road was the next target. The gates were smashed down and the operatives agreed to stop work immediately. Though they left the mill they refused to travel with the mob to Swainson, Birley and Turton's mill, the 'Big Factory', further down London Road. Mr Turton, the joint owner, tried to placate the agitators by promising to release his employees as soon as the dinner break arrived, but the crowd was in no mood to listen. 'No, no,' some of the men shouted, 'Damn that Turton, we will not give him a minute.' The violence escalated: a volley of stones smashed several windows in the watch-house and the entire workforce streamed out of the mill. Constable Walton, who was standing back and observing these events, was attacked. He managed to escape with only slight injuries, but his assistant, Nuttall, was so viciously beaten that immediate medical attention was sought.

Intent on stopping every cotton mill in Preston, the gang of operatives proceeded to Fishergate, *en route* attacking Davis & Co.'s mill in Water Street (where they discovered the hands had already left). The cluster of mills in the Pitt Street area was the next objective. At Clayton and Helm's Ribble Street factory, despite Mr Helm's desperate attempts to negotiate, many windows were broken and the mill engine disabled. John Parks' adjoining factory suffered a similar fate, as did the foundry of Earl Balcarres nearby. Robert Gardner's Kay Street mill, close to Marsh Lane, hastily shut down, followed by those of Oxendale and Rodgett. The final mill to be visited was that owned by Mr Hinksman who, after lengthy discussions with the protesters, which resulted in him receiving a minor injury, reluctantly agreed to release his workforce. Mr Paley, owner of Heatley Street mill, engaged in protracted negotiations with the leaders of the mob, but this was fruitless and his employees were duly turned out. At the Canal Street mill of Horrocks & Co., the men, who were now armed with cudgels, discovered the factory gate to be firmly locked. After spending some time trying to batter the gate down, a group eventually gained entry through the watch-house, and rushed into the mill yard. The main gate was opened and the mob surged through. A barrage of stones was thrown at the factory windows, while several men made for the engine house and put the mill engine out of action by accelerating its speed so that it was seriously damaged. As at other places, some of the operatives joined the hostile band, though many others were reluctant to do so. A cry went up, 'To the moss, to the moss', and the crowd headed towards the Spittals Moss mill of Horrocks & Co. There, once again, the hands came out. During the course of the day, large numbers of townspeople had joined the protesters and the whole group now headed back to the centre of town. As they marched along Friargate they displayed banners, one bearing the words HUNT'S VOLUNTEERS, and the youths, armed with sticks and clubs, began waving these weapons in a formidable manner.

Considerable alarm spread through the town. As the men reached the market square an apple stall was deliberately overturned, and some individuals forced their way into the lock-up and released the only prisoner, a young boy who had been arrested for petty theft. Some ledger books were destroyed and an attempt to burn down the building was only prevented by the intervention of several people living nearby. Once again, attention turned to the Horrocks & Co. Stanley Street works, which had been visited by the mob earlier in the day. Just before 4 p.m., Mr Miller, a senior partner at the mill, came out to meet the crowd with the intention of starting a dialogue, but was unable to make himself heard among the general shouting and jeering. Some misunderstanding antagonised the more violent of the protesters and Miller was repeatedly struck with sticks on the head and shoulders and received considerable bruising to the arm. The crowd rushed into the mill yard, where an employee named Walmsley was attacked with sticks, as was an overlooker called Richard Booth. The workforce left the mill, but then rumours circulated that the employees of Swainson, Birley & Turton had returned to work at Fishwick. The huge crowds, said to have filled the whole length of road from Church Street to the William IV public house, descended London Road to Fishwick mill. The watch-house was stoned, smashing almost every window, while the interior doors and surrounding woodwork were also smashed to pieces. Even the window frames, front and rear, were kicked out, leaving the outside of the building a wreck. A quantity of cotton cloth was seized, ripped to pieces and dragged through the mud and an estimated fifteen dozen top rollers were carried off.

The damage inflicted at Fishwick mill was thus considerable, but with the level of violence increasing the rioters charged back again to Church Street. A gentleman who was simply passing by was singled out as an informer, surrounded and beaten. He managed to find refuge in a nearby timber yard, locking himself in, but his pursuers broke down the door, forcing him back onto the street, and drove him along with sustained blows. The rioters now faced the prison at the corner of Church Street, where a plan was conceived to attack the gaol and free the prisoners inside – estimated to number some 170. Crowbars were procured from the nearby timber yard and the gates of the boundary wall on the west side of the prison were forced by the ringleaders. Several thousand rioters stormed through the gates, advancing towards the prison entrance. The governor of the gaol and a small company of soldiers took up defensive positions. Armed men were placed inside the entrance at the loophole windows on each side of the door, while other soldiers appeared on the roof. As the forward elements of the attackers came within earshot the governor presented his pistol, and the soldiers levelled their muskets at the protesters. Stepping forward, the Governor shouted out, 'If you come to this door, I will shoot you as dead as a robin'.

Faced with this threat, the mob hesitated, noticing the muskets aimed in their direction. They wavered, and began to retreat from the prison grounds. It was a sensible choice, for had the attack continued significant loss of life was inevitable. Apart from a considerable amount of musketry, Captain Anthony of the prison guard had prepared for this emergency by placing a cannon just inside the entrance. Many rioters began to disperse, although the authorities were still anticipating further attacks on private property and, as a precautionary measure, most of the town's shops had closed. In a tense Preston, the severity of the winter weather now dictated events. The night became very cold, with frequent stormy showers, and the principal thoroughfares cleared. Although small knots of men and youths continued to congregate, no more violence was reported and the day's troubles were finally over.

The Reform Act became law in 1832, but even though the electorate increased by over 50 per cent, the principal beneficiaries were the middle classes. The dream of Henry Hunt and other radicals was not to be realised for three more generations. For many radicals, the Reform Act of 1832 was designed simply to appease the reasonably affluent, but previously disenfranchised population. To the working classes, it was largely meaningless. Nevertheless, the long struggle for universal suffrage had begun. Henry Hunt remained an MP only until 1833 and he died in 1835, his dream unachieved.

CHAPTER FOUR

The Spinners' Strike of 1836–1837

IN 1834, in the village of Tolpuddle in Dorset, six farm labourers were arrested for swearing men into a trade union. Although unions had been legal since 1824, the tradition of insisting that new members pledge a secret oath was construed by the authorities as seditious. Despite the trivial nature of the offence, the six were sentenced to seven years' transportation to Australia. After two years of unprecedented campaigning, the 'Tolpuddle Martyrs' were pardoned in 1836. In that year, Preston trade unionists became involved in their own struggle. For some time there had been bitterness among Preston cotton operatives because of wage rates. It seemed that employers in similar cotton manufacturing towns paid far higher wages to their operatives. The Preston cotton masters countered this argument by claiming that the town's geographical position, away from the coalfields and the distribution centre of Manchester, meant far higher transport and production costs. The spinners' union in Preston demanded an increase in wages to achieve the rates being paid in Bolton.

The Preston employers offered a 10 per cent increase which, they said, would raise levels almost to those of Bolton, on condition that the operatives disbanded their union. The spinners responded that even with this increase wages would still fall well short of those in Bolton, and that if the claim was not met in full, together with recognition of the union, a protracted dispute would be inevitable. Another cause of antagonism between employers and operatives was the termination of employment. An employer could dismiss a worker at any time, without reason or prior notice, but an employee had to provide substantial notice when leaving employment. Many workers were tied to complicated contracts that were difficult to terminate and any operative ignoring these restrictions faced substantial fines or even imprisonment.

Such a case was presented to the town's magistrates in October 1836, when five spinners employed at Mr Caton's Back Lane mill were charged with terminating their employment without serving the required notice. The five offered to return and work the remainder of the term, but Caton refused to have them back, insisting that the spinners should each pay him 12 shillings (60 pence) for part payment of losses allegedly sustained through their absence, or be imprisoned. The magistrates offered the men one week to decide on which option they preferred. A similar case appeared the following week, when a woman named Ann Wareing was sentenced to fourteen days in the House of Correction for leaving the spinning mill of Mr Ellis without working out the required notice. Such harsh judgements inflamed an already delicate situation. Another source of hostility was recruitment, which was directed, if possible, towards non-union labour. Before 1836 the membership of the Preston cotton spinners' union was estimated to be between 250 and 300, much less than half the number employed in the trade in the town. In 1836 a successful recruitment campaign resulted in another 350–400 new members joining the organisation. The union was now a force to be reckoned with. The union appears to have reorganised its internal structure in that year, which may help to explain the sudden surge in membership.

By the end of October, serious differences emerged between the proprietors and the operatives, with the masters still determined to resist the demands of their employees. The spinners decided that their absolute determination to achieve their objectives would, if necessary, be reinforced by a complete 'turn out', or strike, by the entire Preston membership. This announcement caused apprehension among the employers, so much so that in the following week some masters, anxious to avoid a damaging dispute, awarded a 10 per cent advance in wages to their spinners. Not all responded likewise, though, and in a remarkable display of solidarity and loyalty towards their workmates the minority of men who received the new rates handed the money back two days later, pledging one for all and all for one. This act of unselfishness made it clear that only a substantial wage increase to *all* the spinners could avert a strike. In any protracted dispute up to 15,000 workers would be affected if, as widely expected, the employers responded to the threat by closing the town's mills and countering a 'turn out' with a 'lock out'.

The industrial action began on 7 November 1836, when all the town's cotton mills, numbering almost thirty, came to a complete standstill with gates locked and thousands of operatives forced out of work. Though there were probably only 650–700 spinners, the impact was far more widespread. Cotton manufacturing involved many different processes, each dependent on the others so, without spinning, everything else came to a halt. Only the spinners, as skilled workers, could exert any pressure on the masters – those in the less skilled trades, heavily reliant on women, children and casual labour, could be hired and fired at will. Hardly unionised at all in 1836, these unskilled workers were nevertheless badly affected by the dispute. On the day the dispute began, a mass meeting of operatives was held at which the spinners reiterated there determination and passed a series of resolutions demanding the 10 per cent increase with full trade union recognition. Ominously, on the previous day tensions had been raised when the military arrived in Preston – 31 soldiers of the 1st Dragoon Guards commanded by Captain Tyson and a company of 55 men of the 7th Fusiliers led by Captain Hamilton and Lieutenant Mildmay. The authorities, anticipating violence, were determined to enforce control.

The dispute dragged on, and in the third week an amicable settlement appeared as far away as ever. The *Preston Chronicle* urged both parties to adopt a more conciliatory attitude and called for an independent tribunal to be established. The newspaper also suggested that the arguments put forward by the masters and the spinners should be supported by factual evidence wherever possible. When examining this evidence, suggested the *Chronicle*, the tribunal must reach a decision based on fairness, decency and common sense, and its conclusions should be binding to both parties. This sensible view was ignored, and the two sides remained entrenched in their original positions. During the fourth week of the stoppage the propaganda campaign escalated. At the beginning of December, many of the millowners announced that they were considering the conversion of existing spinning machinery to automatic operation (or 'self acting' as it was termed). The spinners could not decide whether this was a ploy by the employers to test their resolve, or something more substantial, but it was certain that the introduction of self-acting machinery during a strike would dominate any negotiations with the union. The employers would be able to recruit less skilled operatives and, more importantly, pay less. The *Chronicle* reported this development on 3 December:

Many of the cotton masters in Preston and the surrounding neighbourhood, keen on adapting some of their existing mule machines to the self acting principal, are now in negotiations with Messrs Sharp and Roberts company of Manchester who have successfully patented the new self actors and have seen their installation meet with great advantage by the purchasers. Conversion of the old machines to adapt the new technology can be carried out for a small outlay … The chief object of this conversion, as we understand from the cotton masters, is to employ adults such as hand loom weavers and piecers as attendants at a wage rate currently higher than what they obtain at present and which would compensate the earnings lost with the introduction of the recent Factory Act, which prevents those adults from sending their children into the manufactories. Although no self-acting machine had yet been introduced in Preston, the supposed intentions of the masters to recruit handloom weavers to work on the new machinery had major implications for the Preston spinners. The basic self-actor was perfected by Richard Roberts of Manchester in 1825 and further improved by him with a second patent in 1830. Instead of winding the mule carriage in and out continuously by the use of a hand wheel, the self-actor automated this task. Previously, a spinner required considerable dexterity when operating the machinery, only gained with long practice. Now, though, the spinners feared that the new machinery would be used to exploit them, and would undermine their skilled status.

By mid-December tremendous hardship was apparent throughout Preston, and the Corporation met to consider giving relief and assistance to the unemployed. It was pointed out that of the estimated 15,000 people out of work, only about 7,000 were receiving any kind of assistance. The rest were experiencing acute distress, exacerbated by the harsh winter weather. Some free soup was being distributed at a number of locations about the town, but only on a casual basis, and this was quite inadequate 'to sustain the necessities of life'. Many of the handloom weavers (whose plight was desperate even before the dispute began) were destitute because of the near-impossibility of procuring yarn. When small amounts from other areas did become available, the yarn would be woven round the clock but the cloth was sold on for a miserable 1s. 2d.* per piece. The town council heard the details of acute suffering, such as a family who, despite careful management, had had to pawn everything they possessed and survived on two small meals a day of potatoes, buttermilk and oatmeal. The council was urged to alleviate the suffering of those unconnected with the dispute and to appeal for public donations during the emergency.

Councillor Mitchell recalled with great sadness the grief and misery he had personally witnessed in his own shop, with people absolutely starving, and emphasised the need to act quickly with the proposed public relief fund. He described how young women were resorting to prostitution after pawning nearly every decent article of clothing they had. When he asked these unfortunate girls if they had considered approaching the 'paupers' office', they

---

* 1s. 2d. = 6p. In old-style currency before the decimalisation of sterling in the early 1970s, there were 12 pence (12d.) in 1 shilling (1s.), and 20 shillings (20s.) in £1. Throughout this book old-style money is given in the form £1 16s. 8d.

had all refused. Mitchell knew that they would sooner face death itself than face the grim tyrant who had been placed in charge of that office. The men, he continued, were good men who would willingly exist on a meagre diet of potatoes. Surely, therefore, the town council could afford a donation of £100, with the mayor taking the lead in the public appeal.

As Christmas approached, the struggle between the millowners and spinners continued and hundreds of local families were reported to be in a state of absolute destitution. The strike was now six weeks old but the spinners remained united and there were no reports of a drift back to work. The entire cotton industry of Preston was shut down. Another meeting of the various operatives again pledged constant support for the cotton workers, and the speeches repeated the message of resistance towards what they considered the tyranny of the cotton masters. With the suffering in Preston increasing daily, the spinners sought assistance from outside the town. In Blackburn, a crowded meeting of trade unionists was held to organise financial aid for the Preston operatives. A Preston delegate urged the people of Blackburn to be as generous as they possibly could, while politely reminding the audience that the duty of working men everywhere was to assist one another in such struggles. The same delegate also referred to the plight of the handloom weavers, pointing out that competition among the manufacturers by driving prices down, together with the absence of an organised union, had greatly contributed to their distress. He finished by praising his own men for the peaceful and sober way they had conducted themselves during the painful dispute. Before the meeting dispersed, a resolution was passed in which the trade unionists of Blackburn promised all possible assistance to their Preston colleagues.

Meanwhile, the establishing of a fund to help the operatives was discussed at a public meeting at the Corn Exchange. Joseph Livesey, the well-known reformer, emphasised that the purpose of the meeting was not to debate the perceived rights or wrongs of the strike, but to alleviate the suffering of those unfortunately out of work but unconnected with the spinners. He expressed disappointment at the noticeable absence of the more affluent townspeople from the meeting, and called on all men – regardless of politics, social status, or religion – to support the proposed fund. Livesey was particularly concerned that if the levels of suffering continued, the peaceful nature of the strike could change dramatically. Father Connell of St Wilfred's church agreed that relief for the operatives must come quickly. The suffering, he said, was real and extensive – if remedial steps were not taken promptly, it could prove to be a prelude to even greater horrors. Councillor Mitchell, who had done so much to persuade the mayor and town council to start a public fund, also addressed the

The Corn Exchange, Preston, 1824.
LRO, DDPR 138/27

meeting. He said that if everyone had witnessed what he had seen the previous day, they would have been saddened by the absence of the more influential citizens of the town. Fathers who once were strong, healthy and happy, were now despairing and destitute; mothers were distracted; and daughters once clean, respectable, intelligent, and bearing every mark of virtue, were begging in the streets after dark and when words failed them, had only floods of tears in their appeal for bread.

It was agreed that a committee be formed to administer the relief fund, consisting of town councillors and church ministers. Councillors from each ward would act as collectors for the fund, together with volunteers who might come forward. The donation of £100 from Corporation funds was overwhelmingly approved. There was also debate about the possibility of mediating in the strike in a manner acceptable to both parties. The situation was now so critical for the operatives and for the local economy in general that a way had to be found to end the stalemate. It was agreed to elect a deputation of independent men agreeable to both sides, who would then approach the employers and spinners separately in the hope that common ground could be achieved and full negotiations started. Then, dramatically, two men left their seats and approached the platform. They were recognised by the audience as striking spinners, and greeted with rousing cheers. One of them, James Leeming spoke, agreeing that an impartial deputation could do no harm but added that 'We simply want justice and a fair deal, with nothing more and nothing less. Let the masters show reason and we will give up the dispute, but not before and let them prove to us through mediation that they can show reason.'

So, the first tentative steps had been taken towards negotiation and a possible settlement. But though the meeting at the Corn Exchange ended on an optimistic note, hopes were soon dashed, for shortly afterwards the masters announced their refusal to recognise any suggested deputation or to enter into negotiations. No serious violence or intimidation had yet been reported in Preston, but there was a great deal of crime because, with deprivation and squalor evident almost everywhere, thefts were frequent. Simply keeping warm was an overriding consideration for some of the poorest people, as in the week before Christmas 1836 when three individuals were committed to the House of Correction charged with stealing fuel. Robert Jackson had taken two pieces

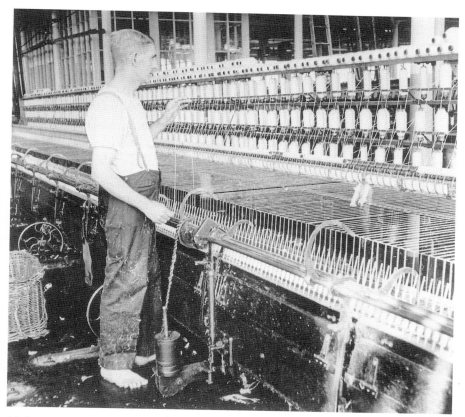

Mule spinning at the Yard Words, c.1920. Spinners such as these were the aristocrats of the cotton industry.

of timber from the Dog Inn on Church Street, while Richard Jenkinson and Richard Slater had stolen a quantity of coal in Penwortham. Begging in Preston had also grown alarmingly, as had the workhouse population. In the New Year of 1837 the masters changed tactics, promising to reopen the mills to anyone who wished to return to work. A promise of an immediate 10 per cent wage increase was on offer to each returning operative, provided that certain conditions were met. Each worker had to sign a written declaration that while in employment at any of the Preston mills, he or she would not at any time become a member of any trade union or combination of workpeople.

With this announcement, the first cracks appeared in the solidarity of the operatives. On 9 January 1837 many cardroom hands, who had received no money since the beginning of the dispute nine weeks previously, went back to work. But the spinners, though their funds were rapidly dwindling, remained firm. Each spinner received 5s. strike pay per week from the union. Their assistants, known as the piecers, received 2s. weekly strike pay but also refused to return to work, as did some of the other ancillary trades, receiving 3s. Sensing that total victory was possibly in sight, the masters began to circulate advertisements offering to train other operatives as cotton spinners. One week after the reopening of the mills, forty spinners were at work, of whom eighteen were non-union men, and the remaining 22 were men who offered to be trained in this skill. With over half of the town's cotton mills now working, albeit in a very limited capacity, up to 1,000 strikers picketed the mill of Paley & Son in Heatley Street, where the majority of the strikebreakers were working. These 'knobsticks', as they were then termed, had to be escorted to and from work each day by a party of police. Inevitably, in the face of so much bitterness and hostility, a number of arrests were made. Six people were brought before the magistrates in the second week of January. For example, Thomas Jenkins was charged with having been among a crowd assembled with the intention of intimidating others. He was committed for trial at Lancaster castle. Christopher Taylor was charged with having shouted 'knobsticks' as the strikebreakers were leaving Paley's mill and was sentenced to six weeks' hard labour at the House of Correction. James Melling and William Welch were said to have been among the crowd that congregated at Paley's factory for the purposes of intimidation. After denying the offence the men were committed for trial at Lancaster castle. Other people arrested for similar offences failed to appear at the court, possibly having fled town or gone into hiding. In a separate incident that same week, Ann Barker, a mechanic's wife, was charged with throwing a stone at a strikebreaker on his way to work. The man had been recruited to learn the spinning trade at one of the Horrocks mills, but the evidence was contradictory and the court ordered the matter to be settled privately. Her husband eventually paid costs as well as 5s. compensation to the strikebreaker. Joseph Higham was charged with assaulting a strikebreaker named Miller as he left Frenchwood mill, but flatly denied the offence, claiming he was simply pushed into Mr Miller and did not hit him. Several witnesses called on his behalf supported him but he was found guilty and ordered to pay a fine of £1 with costs, or serve two months in prison.

In each case the magistrates expressed their determination to protect those who chose to work and to punish severely anyone attempting to assault or intimidate those individuals. By 16 January three union spinners had returned to work, and a further sixty operatives volunteered to be trained as spinners. One week later came another blow for the union, when forty men brought in from neighbouring towns began to operate the spinning machines in the town. It was also known that two Preston mills (probably Rodgett's in Bow Lane and Dawson's Aqueduct Street premises) had purchased several of the new self acting spinning machines. As the number of working machines increased, there were more ancillary workers tempted to break the strike and return. Barker's mill, in an effort to entice their spinners back, dropped the ultimatum which required operatives to sign a declaration renouncing trade union membership or activity. Within days, all of Barker's spinners had returned to work. The majority of Preston spinners as yet remained steadfast, but these events were a huge setback for the union. Following the events at Barker's mill, and in a final effort to break the strike, the masters agreed to modify the terms of the required declaration if a mass return to work was forthcoming. The unions rejected this proposition out of hand, insisting on their original demands, and this in turn provoked the masters to announce an intention of recruiting non-union labour. The employers were convinced that the strike was crumbling, but were experiencing difficulties. A substantial number of spinning machines were now operating, but the piecers, who were needed to reconnect broken threads during the spinning process, had remained largely loyal to the union. The Fishwick mill in London Road, in particular, had this problem: they could obtain enough men to operate the machines, but could not attract the required number of piecers.

Another meeting was held in the town, at which delegates from various cotton manufacturing centres addressed the packed audience. Trade unionists from Manchester, Stockport, Bolton, and Ashton-under-Lyne, as well as local men, urged the operatives to remain steadfast. The delegates promised to return to their districts and raise more funds, to carry the Preston operatives through the dispute. But locally the position was deteriorating rapidly. Non-union labour was being recruited to the town's mills and a steady stream of local operatives abandoned the struggle. Because of enormous rent arrears among the strikers, many faced eviction. The union had already spent £900 from its bank balance, and the public fund set up by the council had provided little assistance. Another demoralising factor was the continuing number of arrests among union supporters. In late January 1837 Thomas Pearson, a cotton piecer loyal to the union, was charged with assaulting a strikebreaking spinner. The evidence presented appeared flimsy and the magistrates were about to discharge Pearson, when suddenly fresh evidence was supplied by the arresting officer. Despite vehemently denying the new accusations, Pearson was convicted and fined 30s. or imprisonment with hard labour for one month. Other union supporters were brought before the magistrates on charges of intimidation and though the evidence was often scanty, each case led to conviction.

The strike was now almost thirteen weeks old, and the determination of the union started to disintegrate. During the week beginning 5 February 1837 the striking Preston operatives reluctantly returned to work. Although some of the millowners awarded the 10 per cent wage increase, the strike was effectively lost. Wages rates in Preston were still inferior to those of the Bolton spinners, and trade union recognition, for which the Preston operatives had fought so tenaciously for three months, was as far away as ever. The weary spinners, on their return to work, had to endure the vindictiveness of some of the maters, who systematically set out to weed their workforce of activists. In a statement issued by the Association of Preston Master Spinners shortly after the end of the strike, the attitude of the employers was made very clear. As the *Preston Chronicle* reported, all spinners in Preston and neighbourhood would henceforth be expected to sign the following declaration before witnesses:

> I [name] do hereby solemnly declare that I am not now, nor so long as I continue in the employ of [name] will I become, a member of, or directly or indirectly, a subscriber of any Trades Union or other combination of men to interfere between masters and workmen.

Even though the operatives were forced into signing this declaration in order to work again, it did not guarantee employment. According to statistics furnished by the Preston employers after the end of the dispute, of a total of some 650 spinners engaged in the mills before its outbreak, only 367 were allowed to return to work. The rest were replaced with 'blackleg' labour, and over 250 were summarily dismissed and blacklisted by the masters, with no hope of future employment in Preston mills. William Ainsworth, the secretary of the employers' association, wrote on 3 March 1837 that 'The masters are now as fully determined as ever to allow no Trades Unionist amongst their men, or to admit of foreign dictation in the management of their affairs'. For the 250 or so spinners and activists now unemployed, the only hope of work was either to take a job totally unconnected with the cotton trade, or to work in another cotton town. For many, though, even the latter option was unrealistic, as their reputation often preceded them, and the blacklisting network could be extensive.

In the journal *The Working Man's Companion*, published in 1838, it was stated that twelve trade unionists or sympathisers were imprisoned or held on bail for assaults or intimidation. About twenty young women became prostitutes (and over half of these carried on that trade after the strike) and two of these unfortunates were consequently transported to Australia for theft. Three people were believed to have died from starvation. In most families in Preston connected with the dispute and lock out, almost every item of clothing and household furniture was pawned and in nine houses out of ten considerable rent arrears had accumulated and were due for repayment instantly. Trade union loyalists were not the only ones singled out after the strike. Two of the Masters Association's own members, Messrs T. and J. Barker, and Mr Richard Bashall, were formally expelled from the organisation for refusing to insist that operatives sign the anti-union declaration. The first major confrontation between the employers and the workforce had ended in defeat for the spinners.

Nevertheless, many of their prominent members were unemployed and blacklisted, and their organisation was broken and almost bankrupt, the spinners' union would eventually recover. In time, other men would come forward with exactly the same ideals as the men who had challenged the power of the masters in 1836. The movement in Preston would gradually expand and move forward, as operatives in other cotton trades, as well as the spinners, realised the advantages of combination, and formed organisations of their own.

CHAPTER FIVE

Chartism and the tragedy of 1842

FOLLOWING THE COLLAPSE of the spinners' strike in 1837, and with the Preston Union struggling for survival, agitation took a new direction. Leading radicals combined to form a new movement for political reform. It was known as Chartism, and its followers as Chartists, because the movement (officially launched in Birmingham in August 1838) had as its focus the 'People's Charter', which set out the proposed reforms: annual parliaments; universal male suffrage; equal electoral districts; an end to property qualifications for MPs; voting by secret ballot; and payment for MPs (so that they were not dependent upon personal wealth).

The Preston Radical Association, formed in 1837, soon had 200 members and quickly aligned itself with the Chartists. The movement son gathered support among middle-class radicals and working people alike, while a trade recession after 1836 encouraged many disaffected workers to join the cause. Chartism seemed to many ordinary folk to be a path to genuine change and a good number of Preston people embraced these ideals as enthusiastically as they had trade unionism. A rally in Preston was arranged for 5 November 1838, at which Feargus O'Connor, the celebrated leader of the Chartists, was to be the speaker. Handbills and placards announced the meeting well in advance, and over 2,500 people assembled (near the site of the former Preston Hospital at Deepdale). About 500 had marched from Blackburn to join the demonstration and eight musical bands were present, with almost forty banners. Many of these displayed radical slogans such as 'Universal Suffrage, Equal Rights And Equal Laws', and 'Better To Die By The Sword Than Perish With Hunger'. One bore the message 'Justice to Ireland' and, in an obvious reference to a recent infamous event, one depicted the Peterloo Massacre of 1819. Feargus O'Connor mounted the platform together with other delegates from the Chartist movement, accompanied by Alderman Noble from Preston and the speeches began. Richard Marsden, a handloom weaver and well known radical from Bamber Bridge, delivered a scathing attack on the way parliamentary legislation treated ordinary folk. Quoting the New

Poor Law as an example, he heavily criticised legislation which 'meant that poor people could be locked up in dungeons simply because they could not find employment'. However, the People's Charter was the main theme of a succession of speakers. The meeting was counted a huge success.

The Chartists presented a petition to parliament in July 1839, calling for extensive reform. It was said to have been signed by over 1,200,000 people, but parliament rejected it out of hand. Incensed by this rebuff, the Chartists gradually became more fragmented. Some of the more extreme elements proposed an armed insurrection, but for a time the majority continued to pursue the goal of peaceful change. In May 1842, almost four years after the movement had been formed, a further petition was presented to parliament by Feargus O'Connor. This time it was allegedly signed by more than 3 million people and was said to be six miles long. It again called for universal male suffrage, and other democratic reforms, but after debating the Peoples Charter the House of Commons rejected it by 287 votes to 49. For many people this second rejection was insupportable. In early August 1842 a minor dispute by cotton operatives at Ashton-under-Lyne led to major industrial unrest. Within days, the Manchester operatives left work proclaiming a strike for the charter. Word soon spread, and workers in various trades struck in the Midlands, Cheshire, Yorkshire, Wales and the Scottish coalfields. Some militant elements called for an immediate insurrection, and nationally the situation became very threatening. Preston became embroiled in this spontaneous eruption of anger, culminating unfortunately in a tragedy that would scar the town for many years to come.

On Friday 12 August 1842 the powerloom weavers employed at Ainsworth's Church Street mill met at Chadwick's Orchard (the present site of the market in Orchard Street) early in the morning. The meeting was intended to discuss an internal dispute at the mill, but Chartist sympathisers and agitators either from among Ainsworth's weavers, or who had infiltrated the meeting, urged the operatives to stop work immediately and to strike in sympathy with workers in other areas. About three hours later, a group of men marched from Friargate to Paley's mill in Heatley Street and demanded that the workforce should join the demonstration. The mill manager, fearing violence, brought the works to a halt. The men then went to Marsh Lane and Pitt Street, where the mills of Gardner and Park were stopped. Mr Rodgett, owner of the Bow Lane mill, learned of the intentions of the crowd and ordered the gates to be securely locked. As the mob approached his premises, he attempted to reason with them, but some began battering the mill gates, and others climbed the walls into the yard. They threatened to wreck the entire mill, and so Rodgett reluctantly agreed to discharge his workforce. Other mills in Arthur Street, Bow Lane and Pitt Street were similarly brought to a standstill. Oxendale's mill in Cable Street, and the workshops of German and Newsham, were then stopped.

The crowd carried on to the two Horrockses mills, in Canal Street and Fylde Road, where they smashed open the gates and ordered the employees out on the street, and then repeated the action at Dawson's factory further along Fylde Road. At Taylor's old Tulketh mill, near the canal basin at Shelley Road, the employees were slow in responding to the ultimatum, so the demonstrators forcibly entered the premises, threatened the workforce and demanded that they leave immediately. There were only two constables in the area and they could only follow the crowd and try to ascertain the identities of the ringleaders. The constables were threatened and so maintained a discreet distance as the rioters proceeded along Aqueduct Street to Dawson's weaving sheds, McGuffog's mill in Brook Street, and Hawkins' mill in Adelphi Street. By then, however, the police had assembling a more formidable force of officers, so the agitators, now numbering over 500, decided to separate from the main group of demonstrators who were heading back toward the centre of town.

At every cotton mill, machine shop or factory believed to be still at work, the mob descended. Thus, at the mill of German, Petty & Co., it was rumoured that several cotton reelers had continued working, so the rioters forced open the gates and began smashing the windows, until the few remaining terrified employees left their work. Once satisfied that every major manufacturer in Preston had been forced to stop production, the mob, estimated to be about 3,000-strong, returned to the Orchard. Chartist speakers urged the Preston workers to continue their support for the strike that was sweeping through the manufacturing districts of Lancashire and beyond. The minor individual dispute at Ainsworth's mill had grown into a strike for the Charter, and the town was in a very tense state. The local police and magistrates, unable to cope with the situation, relayed urgent messages to Blackburn and Wigan calling for military assistance. Meanwhile, anticipating serious violence, the artillery piece inside Preston prison had been mounted in readiness, and the small company of soldiers stationed there was on full alert. Some 21 soldiers arrived from Blackburn, and a further fourteen from Wigan came by special train early in the evening.

Everyone nervously awaited the following day. On the evening of 12 August the magistrates held a meeting at the Bull and Royal Hotel in Church Street to assess the situation, while the 72nd Highlanders remained under arms the

CHARTISTS' RIOTS.

Chartists' riots, from a later engraving.

entire night. The mill owners also held a meeting, at which they decided to reopen the mills for the Saturday morning shift. They hoped that the day's events would not be repeated. Early the following day, Saturday 13 August 1842, the cotton mills reopened for work again. Large groups of demonstrators assembled at the Orchard, but soon left for Francis Sleddon's Hanover Street mill near North Road. Sleddon was already at the premises and was in no mood to be dictated to by the crowd. His employees turned the water hoses on the visitors, who retaliated by smashing the mill windows. Several people were hurt, among them Sleddon himself, and soon the workforce had evacuated the mill. Catterall's mill near Sedgwick Street was also stopped when rioters forced their way into the yard, then into the engine house, where they disabled the machinery. The magistrates, learning of these developments, decided to mobilise the military and police in order to confront and then disperse the rioters, who were now moving towards the mills along the canal. As the military headed along Fishergate, the vanguard of the rioters emerged from

Lune Street. On seeing the soldiers, they cleared the road and hurried onto the footpaths. Perhaps fearing that they were being surrounded, the officer in command ordered his men to halt and form a new line stretching across the entire street.

As the troops formed up, the rioters pelted them with stones. Captain Woodford moved towards them, as if trying to calm the situation, but a young man urged the main body of demonstrators forward to confront the soldiers. Woodford attempted to arrest him, and a scuffle broke out in which the chief constable was punched to the floor and kicked. The troops and police then advanced down Lune Street, driving the rioters before them. Some of the mob began to disperse but the main body of rioters halted down the street and again stoned the police and soldiers. Women and children who had accompanied the protesters supplied the men with stones from large piles that lay nearby beside the canal basin. The troops and police, halfway down Lune Street, faced several hundred rioters who were at the bottom of the slope close to Fleet Street. The mayor stepped forward, to persuade the rioters to disperse and to read out the Riot Act. He was met with a barrage of stones, one of which knocked the document from his hand. A large body of men broke away from the main group, ran up Fox Street to Fishergate, and approached the troops and police from behind. Standing at the top of Lune Street, they pelted them with stones and hemmed them in. The soldiers turned to face this new threat, the stone-throwing ceased, and the mayor again approached the main body of protesters, urging them to see reason and disperse. He could not make himself heard amid the general noise, and was then struck on the leg with a stone. The fateful order was given to the troops to open fire.

Contemporary reports suggest that a rumour swept through the demonstrators that they had nothing to fear because the military had only been issued with blanks. A man named John Mercer advanced towards the soldiers, armed with stones and raising his arm to throw one. The soldiers opened fire, hitting Mercer. He staggered to the pavement, fell, then rolled over apparently dead. Several other rioters were also hit by the volley of shots. For a moment after the firing, the rioters appeared transfixed with disbelief as to what had just happened, and some time passed before anyone went to assist Mercer and the other victims. Eventually, as the reality of the tragedy unfolded, the crowd dispersed, taking the dead and wounded with them. A number of the more seriously injured were taken to the House of Recovery at Deepdale with musket ball wounds, while others were taken directly to their homes.

Four people died. George Sowerbutts was a nineteen-year-old weaver from Chandler Street, employed at Gardner's mill in Marsh Lane. He was hit by

a musket ball in the right side of the chest. The ball passed out through his back, breaking and shattering several ribs on its way. He died the following day. Bernard McNamara, a cotton stripper aged seventeen of Birk Street, near Marsh Lane, was employed at Oxendale's mill. He was hit in the lower part of the right side of the stomach. Considerable damage was inflicted to the intestines, with heavy loss of blood and he died two days later. William Lancaster, aged twenty five, died six days after being shot through the chest. John Mercer, a handloom weaver aged twenty-seven, of Ribbleton Lane, received severe wounds to the chest and died shortly afterwards. Other men who received serious injuries were named as Bryan Hodgson (36), a shoemaker of St Paul's Square, wounded in the lower part of the back; Lawrence Pilling (21), a steamloom weaver of Moss Rose Street off Fylde Road, suffered terrible injuries to a leg, the musket ball having seriously splintered the bone, resulting in amputation shortly afterwards; and James Roberts (21), a steamloom weaver of Savoy Street near Marsh Lane, who was employed at Mr Gardner's mill and was shot through the forearm.

After the events of Saturday 13 August 1842, the Preston authorities were absolutely determined that no further similar disturbances would take place in the town. A detachment of the 60th Rifles, and the Wigan troop of the Lancashire Yeomanry, soon arrived. Handbills were posted around the streets banning groups of people from congregating, and informing the townsfolk that any attempts to prevent people from working would have the most serious consequences. As another precautionary measure, all public houses and beer shops were ordered to close their doors at 5 p.m. until further notice. Although rumours circulated that large numbers of disaffected and militant coalminers were about to descend on Preston, the presence of the military and yeomanry ensured that the town remained relatively quiet. Gradually, normality returned, and many in Preston mourned the dead.

CHAPTER SIX

Recession and the
Ten Per Cent question

Despite the tribulations of the late 1830s and early 1840s, the cotton industry in Preston continued to expand. Napier and Goodair's Brookfield mill near North Road opened in 1841, with Gardner and Crankshaw's Moor Park mill in St George's Road following soon after. Lord Street mill began production in the same year and during the years around 1840 McGuffog's Murray Street mill and Dawson's Aqueduct Street site were also completed. Gardner's and Naylor's Oxheys mill, at the junction of Ripon and Brook Street, opened by 1844, while in the same year John and Adam Leigh's Brookhouse mill in Old Lancaster Lane started up. Many Preston masters were now investing in new weaving technology, widening the town's cotton manufacturing base away from a dependence on spinning. However, this period of expansion preceded a decline in trade nationally – by 1846 a severe recession gripped the cotton industry. Such was the distress in Preston by December 1846 that a public meeting was held in the town hall to consider the welfare of the poor, who had been badly affected by the depression. Shock was expressed at the state of the less fortunate townspeople, and it was agreed to open two soup kitchens – one in the area of Church Street, the other in the traditional Irish quarter in Canal Street. Two kinds of soup were made available, with the meat-based variety selling at one penny per quart, and the vegetable at a halfpenny per quart. It was also decided to use the large boiler at St Paul's School in Pole Street, which was capable of boiling one hundred gallons of liquid each day, and another boiler was urgently requested to cater for the expected demand over the forthcoming weeks. A collection at the town hall raised almost £150 for the soup fund and a proposal that the newspaper offices in Preston should open a subscription list for donations was unanimously agreed.

In January 1847, there having been no improvement in trade, a third soup kitchen was set up in a coal yard in Fleet Street. Contemporary statistics indicate that the three soup kitchens distributed almost 450 gallons a day by the end of January. The Poor Law Board of Guardians, who were responsible for the application of relief to the poor, were aware of a significant increase in acute poverty. Workhouses in the district, including those at Preston, Walton-le-Dale, Penwortham, and Woodplumpton, together with the local House of Recovery, reported that there were 820 inmates in total by the end of the month. By May 1847, over 1,000 Preston cotton operatives were unemployed, and another 5,000 were on short time, working four rather than the normal six days each week. Towards the end of October, one in every six of the town's population was in receipt of charitable aid, not including those Prestonians whose plight was so severe that they had been admitted to the workhouse to avoid starvation. On 20 November 1847, the *Preston Guardian* reported on the widespread distress:

> We have consulted those who call at hundreds of the poor people's houses every week, such as collectors for Burial Societies and collectors of rent, and they affirm that the people were never so reduced to poverty and utter destitution as at present. They are leaving their separate dwellings and two or three families are squeezing in to a single cottage. Their all is gone, furniture sold to subsist upon, clothing all worn out.

In September, William Ainsworth the cotton manufacturer had announced a 5 per cent reduction in the wages of his employees at Church Street mill. This shock came less than four months after a similar 5 per cent reduction had been enforced. John Paley junior, another prominent mill owner who was also mayor of Preston, announced similar reductions, and the general opinion was that the majority of the cotton masters would follow suit. The large and well-organised Preston weavers' union immediately protested against this decision, and called a meeting of the membership, but against the background of a trade depression, and with wage reductions in many Lancashire cotton districts, the Preston weavers abandoned any thoughts of action against the employers. The only crumb of hope was the promise made by the masters to restore wages to former levels once trade had sufficiently improved.

Fortunately, by 1849 the Lancashire cotton trade appeared to be moving out of recession. Both the weavers' and spinners' unions decided in Preston, as in other cotton towns, to petition the masters for the full 10 per cent restoration of wages that had been promised prior to the recovery. Expecting that the masters would be reluctant to do so, the unions decided to compromise, indicating that the 10 per cent restoration could be phased over three years.

The millowners denied that any commitment to restore the former wage rates had ever been made, although the unions still believed that the masters were bluffing and would eventually negotiate. By 1852, new spinning and weaving sheds were being built all over Preston and, with full employment again restored, the unions considered that the masters no longer had any excuse to fail to restore the wage cuts. Early in 1853, a planned and coordinated campaign by the unions began to gather considerable momentum throughout Lancashire, as delegates negotiated with the mill owners. By the spring, despite weeks of discussions, no major breakthrough had been achieved, and a confrontation between operatives and employers looked increasingly likely. In early June, sporadic strikes in Stockport developed into a complete stoppage of the town's cotton mills, as the operatives demanded a full restoration of the 10 per cent cut. The great industrial battle that would envelop Lancashire and Preston had begun.

It was essential for the Lancashire unions that the Stockport dispute was successful. If the workers there were starved back to work, the battle for the full restoration of the cuts throughout the county would certainly be lost. Therefore, union delegates from seventeen cotton manufacturing centres met to pledge wholehearted support for the Stockport strikers. In Preston, in July 1853, a meeting of millworkers in support of the operatives in Stockport attracted over 2,000 people. Henry Wilkinson, a prominent activist, read out a list of donations collected for the Stockport hands from the various towns. Stockport itself had raised almost £80, Accrington £60, Preston £50, Darwen £38, Oldham £30, Bolton £28, Hyde £25, Droylsden £19, Bury £15, Ashton-under-Lyne £14, Clitheroe £14, Gorton £10–15, and Blackburn a remarkable £180. The total amount raised was £628 13s. 6d. This enabled the Stockport unions to distribute 2s. each to over 5,000 hands and 1s. each to 5,000 strikers employed as reachers and helpers. George Cowell addressed the meeting, insisting that the mill masters had no justification whatever in resisting the restoration of the 10 per cent. Cowell, a dedicated trade unionist and the recognised leader of the Preston weavers, poured scorn on the employers saying that

If they will rather prove before a jury of disinterested gentlemen of respectability and experience that they are in as bad a position now as when the reductions took place in 1847, we will abandon our claim to a more favoured time. But if they will not submit to reason or arbitration, we have no other course left as English men and women, but to persevere and never rest till we have reached our object. The consciousness that we are performing our

George Cowell
ILLUSTRATED LONDON NEWS, 1853

duty to ourselves, our families, to society at large and to posterity, will
cheer us in our struggle and whatever be the consequences, on their own
heads rests the responsibility. We leave that to posterity and to God.

Following George Cowell's bitter condemnation of the attitude of the
Lancashire cotton employers, tension again increased in Preston, and relations
between the masters and operatives became further strained. On 19 July 1853,
eight weavers employed at Ainsworth's mill were brought before the magistrates

for refusing to work, after one of their colleagues was dismissed for collecting money for the Stockport strikers. The eight, who included Daniel Pearson, Roger Walker, Richard Stanley, Thomas Walmsley, Lawrence Hodgson, Thomas Fletcher, and P. Hesketh, were found guilty. They were liable to three months imprisonment, but Ainsworth's representative did not insist on committal and instead demanded costs. The following evening, an estimated 1,000 operatives gathered at the end of Marsh Lane. George Cowell and two other senior union officials brought news of an incident at Rodgett's Bow Lane mill. Rodgett had informed his weavers that if they were unable to produce fourteen cuts of finished cloth each week, he would deduct one shilling from their wages. Claiming that these targets were a physical impossibility, even without allowing for any breakdown in machinery, the weavers had retaliated by striking until the ultimatum was withdrawn. The operatives were informed of other ominous developments. Several union activists, who had attended previous public meetings outside working hours, had been sacked after being seen collecting for the Stockport hands. Cowell and the rest of the Preston leadership were concerned at the way events were unfolding, and noted that although the Stockport strike remained solid, with over 14,000 operatives on strike, the employers there had still not conceded. Union delegates throughout Lancashire, conscious of the enormous sums required to sustain the Stockport operatives through this fight, were understandably reluctant to expand the dispute for the time being. With this in mind, and recognising the need first to secure victory in Stockport, Cowell urged the strikers at Rodgett's mill to return to work, and called for an end to sporadic sympathy strikes in Preston.

Nevertheless, the confrontational attitude continued in the town over the following weeks. On 14 August a large procession of cotton workers paraded through Preston in support of the 10 per cent restoration. The parade finished at the Orchard where, at the largest meeting held so far in support of the 10 per cent issue and the Stockport strike, George Cowell, with another Preston leader, Edward Swindlehurst, began announcing the amounts so far contributed to the cause. No less than £1,247 7s. 6d. had been collected in the previous week alone, £75 of it from Preston. The people of Blackburn had again displayed extraordinary commitment by raising £345, a testimony to their collective beliefs and trade union solidarity. Then, Swindlehurst announced that the Stockport Cotton Masters Association had agreed to award the full 10 per cent advance to all their spinners and cardroom hands. Although the weavers had only been offered 5 per cent, the delegates firmly believed that in a matter of days they too would receive the full award. The meeting erupted with applause and cheering at this news and the meeting dispersed in a joyful mood. As predicted, two days later the Stockport weavers won the full 10 per cent and the breakthrough of which all Lancashire cotton operatives had dreamed had been achieved. The Stockport strike for the 10 per cent, which had lasted almost two months, was over. It was a great victory.

Following the events in Stockport, Horrocks, Miller & Co., Preston's largest employer, promised to award the full 10 per cent for certain kinds of work, while Swainson and Birley promised the same general advance the following week. Ainsworth & Co., together with Messrs Lawson, Swarbrick and Almond continued this trend, while the company of Napier and Goodair had for some days already been paying the full 10 per cent. Among the other cotton employers no such promises were as yet forthcoming, and it was agreed at a meeting of the manufacturers that each should exercise his own discretion in the matter. It really did appear that the Lancashire cotton union's campaign was meeting with success.

A week later, at a mass meeting of the operatives (estimated by the Preston Guardian to be 10,000 strong), George Cowell described the latest developments in Blackburn. 'I am pleased to announce,' said Cowell, 'that the Blackburn mill masters have conceded the full ten per cent advance and with revised piecework rates, should equate the offer to almost twelve per cent.' The audience was euphoric on hearing this news, and thunderous applause erupted. The following days were as highly charged, as news arrived that the Accrington and Bolton employers had also conceded to the demand. On 20 August the *Guardian* published an official declaration from Burnley, where the masters agreed to award the 10 per cent immediately. There was celebrating throughout the cotton manufacturing districts, and it appeared that the strategy of the combined Lancashire cotton unions had been fully vindicated. By procuring sufficient funds to sustain the Stockport hands through to victory, the rewards had been general, for employers in other towns appeared keen to avoid a similar dispute. The last bastion of resistance was in Preston, where some mill masters were among the most stubborn in the region. In late August 1853 the picture in Preston was confusing. All but five of the town's mills had pledged to award the new rates but, as George Cowell reported, in reality only Horrocks, Miller & Co. and Hawkins had actually been forthcoming with the 10 per cent, and they had limited the rise to the weavers only. The employers had also categorically refused to enter negotiations about equalising Preston rates with those elsewhere in Lancashire.

The patience of the operatives began to evaporate. Intermittent walkouts occurred at several of the town's mills, and at a hastily arranged meeting

Contrast the living conditions of the Preston cotton workers with those of the millowner Thomas Miller, whose house on Winckley Square this was …

PHOTOGRAPH: CARNEGIE, 2007

of union delegates at the Farmers Arms public house, Cowell reported that the attitude of the major cotton employers had, in his opinion, hardened considerably. He told how Thomas Miller, one of the proprietors of the large Horrocks company, had described Preston unionists as 'A set of agitators who are living in idleness upon the pence of the public'. After a lengthy debate the trade delegates resolved that the Preston operatives should pursue their rightful claim for 10 per cent, together with an equalisation of piecework rates. They also unanimously agreed to provide considerable financial support in any forthcoming struggle. Cowell and other local committee members met the following day at the Temperance hall, where another round of serious discussions took place. A resolution was unanimously agreed: 'That it is the opinion of this meeting that as a number of the master cotton spinners of Preston have not acceded to the required advance of ten per cent, the operatives in their employ shall tender into their respective masters their notices this week, which shall be legally served by them according to the rules of the different firms in which they are engaged'.

The sporadic unofficial strikes in the town presented the union with considerable problems and may well have influenced their decision to issue this ultimatum. Eight cotton rovers employed at Walker's Lords mill in Grimshaw Street were summoned to appear at the town hall on Tuesday 23 August, for allegedly leaving their work. They had taken this action after learning that only the weavers employed by Walker would receive the 10 per cent. Five twisters employed at Hawkins' Greenbank mill faced a similar summons after striking over the same issue. There was some good news for the union, when John Gardner, a small manufacturer, informed the Preston committee that he was prepared to pay the full 10 per cent to all his workers, and another employer, John Cooper, promised not only to award the 10 per cent, but also to equalise wages according to a range of prices averaged over a 60-mile radius. Gradually, though, the seriousness of the situation in Preston became more evident. The majority of Preston cotton employers began to prepare for a major confrontation with the unions, and George Cowell issued his celebrated battle cry to his followers: 'The ten per cent movement is one of right and so earnest am I in this struggle, that I would like to embrace the men who stand nobly in this warfare of right against might'.

The cotton employers and the operatives remained defiant. And in the 27 August edition of the *Preston Guardian* an article reported the death at the age of 68 of a cotton worker, Mr Parkinson of Moor Lane, who had worked for 62 years as a mill operative. Such was the harshness of life for ordinary working people in Preston.

CHAPTER SEVEN

The great Preston Lockout of 1853–1854

T HE INDUSTRIAL SITUATION in Preston became ever more fragile during September 1853. The factory hands at Mr Swainson's worsted mill in Leighton Street, no longer prepared to be patient over the 10 per cent question, were already engaged in a total stoppage. Other operatives, with or without union blessing, were also confronting employers, while a major mill owner, Miles Rodgett, bluntly told his workforce that if they were not satisfied with their present wages they could quit the premises. Following this, Mr Orrell, an employer of Walton-le-Dale, notified the union that if Rodgett did not award the 10 per cent, he would withdraw his own offer of the same. The workforce at Swarbrick and Lawson's North Road mill also resolved to withdraw their labour, after the owners reversed the decision to award the new rates. Union delegates from other districts had been busy organising the financial support that would soon be required for the Preston operatives. Accrington had already guaranteed a levy of 3d. per loom, as had the workers of Over Darwen, while Blackburn had promised 2d. per loom with substantial increases if necessary. Many trade delegates felt that the Preston unions needed to press the issue more forcefully, rather than wait for the bigger owners to concede. An understandable concern of the Lancashire delegates was that if many Preston masters refused the 10 per cent, millowners throughout the county would use this as a pretext to withdraw the recent hard won gains.

On the morning of 15 September, following a private meeting at the Bull and Royal, the Preston Master Spinners Association issued a statement in which the employers gave notice that exactly one month hence, every cotton manufactory in Preston would be closed indefinitely. Notice to that effect would be displayed in the mills or given to the workpeople. The employers who had agreed to this action entered into a bond, and any master failing to carry out the plan would immediately forfeit £5,000. Only the company of Slater and Smith of Kent Street mill refused to sign the document, while Napier and Goodair, who owned several mills in the town but were not members of the association, did not attend the meeting. If the Preston cotton workers had been in any doubt over the intentions of the employers, the position was now perfectly clear. From 15 October 1853 the operatives would be locked out.

The next public meeting of the operatives had, coincidentally, been scheduled for the evening of 15 September, at the Orchard. It was to be preceded by a march around town headed by two bands. As the operatives gathered near the Springfield Inn on Marsh Lane, before the parade started at 6.15 p.m., posters prohibiting any such march were being displayed all around the Orchard. The official prohibition read as follows:

> **Caution**: The Mayor and Magistrates of the borough of Preston, being satisfied that the public procession with two bands of music advertised to start from the Springfield Inn, Marsh Lane at a quarter past six o'clock this evening, at which all turn outs are requested to attend, has a direct tendency to a breach of the peace and the intimidation of the inhabitants, hereby forbid such processions and caution all persons from attending the same, as they will answer the contrary at there peril.

Unmoved, the operatives continued with the parade, arriving at the Orchard with both bands playing before settling in readiness for the speeches. George Cowell took the platform and spoke bitterly about the masters' stance, while at the same time urging the operatives to remain calm and peaceful throughout. Prosecutions, declared Cowell, were rife and the strong arm of the law had been called upon to put them down, but these prosecutions had fallen on comparative children, who had been dragged before a bench stuffed with cotton. In a rousing final outburst he said that

> The Queen had said in her recent speech that trade was in a prosperous condition and if they believed what her Majesty said, they must believe they had a right to share in that prosperity. The masters had no excuse for resisting. This was now a struggle between capital and labour'

Towards the end of September 1853, with the deadline for the proposed lockout just over two weeks away, the unions attempt conciliation with the cotton masters. A letter was sent by Thomas Blackburn and John Bowman, the chairman and secretary of the Power Loom Weavers' Committee, to William Ainsworth and Thomas Miller of the masters association. It said that

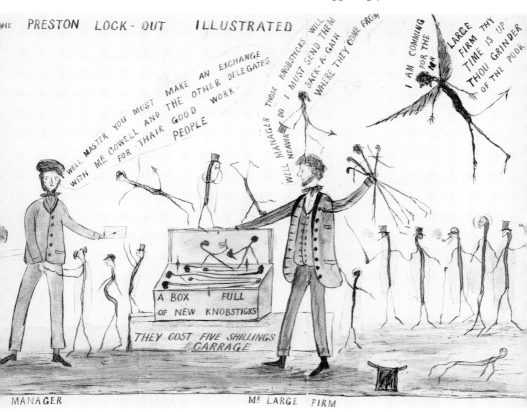

A contemporary cartoon illustrating the role played by strike-breaking 'knobsticks' recruited by millowners such as Ainsworth and Miller.

In order to convince you and the public at large that we are not unreasonable, that we have no desire to dictate to you, or ask you to agree to any terms inconsistent with your station as employers and believing, Gentlemen, that from you holding a high social position in the town, you must desire to see this unfortunate dispute brought to an amicable arrangement. We propose, 1st, that a deputation of employers meet a deputation of the workpeople, for the purpose of discussing and arranging the difference. Or if this were objectionable, we propose 2nd, That the matter in dispute be referred to arbitration, each party to appoint an equal number of experienced men unconnected with the strike and that R.T. Parker, Esquire, M.P, be the umpire. If this does not meet your views, we respectfully request you to make a proposal, if you desire to come to an honourable arrangement, and if it were based on equity, we pledge ourselves to accept it.

Several days later a reply was received:

> The committee of the Masters Association have had laid before them the letter addressed by T. Blackburn and J. Bowman, to Mr Miller and Mr William Ainsworth and are unanimously of the opinion that they cannot acknowledge the Committee of which they represent themselves as the Chairman and Secretary, or their right to interfere in the dispute at present unhappily existing between the operatives and masters of this town.

The day of the lockout dawned, and Prestonians looked on anxiously as the great majority of the town's mills closed their gates indefinitely. The unions, meanwhile, had built up a 'war chest' to fund for the forthcoming struggle. The Blackburn operatives had vowed to run one loom each for their comrades in Preston, while both Stockport and Ashton-under-Lyne promised to raise £200–£300 per week. Chorley's operatives had publicly stated that, rather than see the people of Preston beaten, they would donate one shilling per loom. Further pledges from the other various cotton manufacturing centres were expected. Meanwhile, the cotton masters decided to test the resolve of the operatives to the limit. As the mills closed, the masters intimated that if the operatives would give up their various trade unions, the 10 per cent wage advance could be expected. The masters insisted each individual must sign a binding document renouncing future trade union membership or participation. This tactic was nothing new, as a similar ploy had been used by the employers during the 1836–37 dispute. In reply, the unions organised a rally at the Marsh on 14 October, the day before the lockout. It was attended by upwards of 8,000 operatives. Edward Swindlehurst, the union leader, took the platform and announced bluntly that 'They wish you, my friends, to break with your Committee and destroy your Union. Will you do so? Remember, we can exist no longer than you will it. Now then, let everyone that has confidence in the Committee and the Union hold up their hands.' A forest of raised hands was the answer to the cotton masters. The workers would not give up the union. As the *Preston Guardian* reported, the manufacturers might as well attempt to stay the rising of the sun with their little finger, as to stay the progress of the toilers towards victory.

In 1853, of Preston's 72,000 people, an estimated 25,000 were employed in cotton mills, of which there were almost sixty. The lockout therefore meant that the majority of the workforce were laid off. Only a few employers ignored the lockout and continued to work, among them Slater and Smith, who owned the Kent Street mill and whose workforce had been awarded the 10 per cent.

From the beginning of the dispute, the Preston Union Committee appreciated the significance of the struggle in which it was now engaged. The millowners of Stockport, Blackburn, Darwen and elsewhere had already indicated they would rescind the 10 per cent advance if the Preston masters were successful in resisting it. For the workers it was therefore vital that the Preston millowners were defeated, even if a protracted strike had to be endured. A spinners' delegate, Green, addressed a mass meeting of the operatives shortly after the lockout began and, anticipating a lengthy fight, warned them of the tremendous sacrifices that would have to be made. Rather than submit, he said, they might have to survive on one meal a day. During the second week, subscriptions to the Preston cause were announced. A total of £1,750 12s. 3d. was to be distributed among the operatives, £613 of this having been contributed by the people of Blackburn. The unions divided the donations on a pro rata basis according to wages normally paid when employed. Statistics provided at the start of the dispute listed the number of operatives allocated to each union who were entitled to receive strike pay:

Name of Union	Category of worker	No. relieved	Sub-total
Power Loom Weavers	weavers	7,395	
	winders	848	
	twisters	223	
	dressers	28	
	helpers	815	
	reachers	12	9,321
Spinners and Self-Actors	spinners and minders	843	
	piecers	773	
	bobbiners	762	2,378
Throstle Spinners	hands [general]	439	439
Tape Machine Sizers	hands [general]	51	51
Card Room Hands	hands [general]	1,801	1,801
Power Loom Overlookers	hands [general]	163	163
Total			**14,153**

Note: these figures do not include many others also unemployed as a result of the lockout: those operatives in trades not yet unionised, workers who chose not to be in a union, children not old enough for union membership, or casual labour. Adding those categories produces a figure of over 20,000.

At the beginning of November 1853, at a meeting of the operatives, George Cowell held aloft a copy of the *Daily News*, which had recently been posted on the walls and buildings of Preston in considerable quantities. He mockingly read out a section which stated that the people of Lancashire and Yorkshire had a good and pleasant life, were in receipt of good wages, had cheap food and plenty of work, and were well fed, well clad and well housed. The assembled strikers howled with spontaneous laughter, but Cowell then turned to more serious matters, condemning the tactics of what he termed Preston's 'Millocracy' and implying that only the masters or their supporters would resort to having such articles printed. The meeting ended with a resounding cheer for the people of Blackburn and other areas for their noble support of Preston. As an early settlement of the dispute seemed unlikely, the unions' attitude to the Preston masters became more hostile. Greenough, a local official, heavily criticised some of the prominent cotton manufacturers, declaring that 'The counting house was their Church, the ledger their Bible and money their God', a view echoed by a visiting delegate from Stockport, Rhodes, who said, 'Money is the God of these manufacturers, they hug their gold'.

During the early weeks of the dispute, the Preston Masters Association confidently reported almost total compliance with its recommendation to enforce the lockout, but by November 1853 a number of the smaller manufacturers had conceded the 10 per cent, or were willing to negotiate with the unions. Slater and Smith, together with Napier and Goodair, had refused to join the lockout from the beginning and now other substantial employers were prepared to award the increase. Williamson's North Road mill, Boys' Back Lane mill, Miller and Lancaster's Fletcher Road mill, Robert Gardner's Kay Street mill and Hugh Dawson's new mill on Fylde Road, were all said to be paying the new rates. The unions did not want to continue the dispute with those employers who had broken ranks, so it was agreed that the operatives at these premises could return to work, if they agreed to donate a substantial part of their wages to help those still locked out.

The wider picture was less encouraging. News from Burnley confirmed that many employers there had withdrawn the 10 per cent, over fifty spinning and weaving sheds were closed, and 7,000 operatives forcibly locked out. In Bacup a widespread lockout was being enforced, while at Padiham the cotton manufacturers not only extended the general lockout but also announced that they would only reopen their premises when the employees agreed not to offer any further support to their Preston fellows. The Burnley masters adopted a variant of this strategy, whereby each worker could only resume employment after binding himself or herself to a one shilling per week deduction of pay over a twelve-week period. Should they have been found to contribute to anyone in dispute at any time during the following six months, they would not only forfeit the twelve shillings but would also be liable to two months imprisonment. Funds from the Burnley area dried up overnight as a result, though the Preston unions were able to distribute another £3,750 among the operatives during a fortnight in November. Nevertheless, for some of the townsfolk the harsh reality was destitution. With the lockout almost a month old, the Preston Board of Guardians reported a marked increase in applicants pleading for relief – numbers doubled in not much more than a week. The able-bodied men were put to work on Preston Moor, while many of the elderly and those unable to work were sent to the workhouse.

By mid-November 1853, the lockout had extended to Walton-le-Dale, Farington and Lostock Hall. A total of 46 mills in the Preston area were reported to be completely stopped, and about 23,000 operatives without work. Approximately 5,000 cotton hands were still working, 1400 of them employed by Napier and Goodair, reputedly the second largest cotton business in Preston. Though the dispute had hitherto been largely peaceful, powerful discontent surfaced on Wednesday 16 November, when groups of Preston men were seen roaming the streets of Blackburn. Some had gone there in search of work, while others were reported to be mustering support for the Preston cause. They were overheard singing 'We'll never be content, Till we get the ten per cent'. By early evening, many of these men had congregated outside the Old Bull Inn, Blackburn, where some of the Preston masters were meeting with their colleagues in Blackburn. Boosted by many of the Blackburn operatives, who were coming off shift, the mob soon numbered 4–5,000. As the meeting ended, several Preston millowners and their supporters were spotted by the crowd and although most managed to escape, one young man, a foreman in the employ of Mr Catterall, was badly beaten. Eyewitnesses claimed that he would have been killed, if he had not been fortunate enough to find refuge in a nearby tavern. No such violent incidents had yet occurred in Preston, but the situation was clearly becoming more unpredictable.

On 1 December 1853 the Preston masters issued a statement, for the attention of the operatives. It said that 'Applications for employment will be received at the mills now closed, on and after Monday the 5th of December 1853 from ten o'clock in the forenoon till four o clock in the afternoon'. The rates of pay offered were those in force before the dispute began – and no 10 per cent increase. Only about 200 workers responded to this, not even 1 per cent of the operatives reported to be locked out. The vast majority were still prepared to endure the hardship. At a meeting of the operatives on 10 December, George Cowell ridiculed the intentions of the Preston masters and the failure of their offer. He reported how, despite deputations going about the town promising half a crown a head and in some instances, a meal of broth to go with it, less than two hundred had bothered to register at the mills. Of these, said Cowell, most were unconnected with the dispute, being employed as fire beaters, mechanics, or sweepers. However, he acknowledged that many Preston folk were suffering to an alarming extent and, referring to a recent article in The Times, headed 'Ignorant population are always on the brink of misery, launched a scathing attack on what he perceived as the true causes of poverty:

> The suffering, great as it may be, is not wholly attributable to the present strike. There are scores of Preston families whose wages were so scanty, that they were sunk in the depths of poverty previous to the lock out. Wherever you find an ignorant class you will always find them, hewers of wood and drawers of water. You will always find men of wealth taking advantage of them, grinding them down to the very dust and before this strike commenced, nine tenths of the factory operatives were a week worse than nothing.

Donations for the cause continued to pour in, from bodies as diverse as the Amalgamated Society of Engineers, the Shipwrights and Sail Makers of Liverpool, London's cork-cutters, and the Sheffield metal trades. The battle cry of 'Ten Per Cent and No Surrender' was by now being heard by working people throughout Britain. With almost £3,000 arriving each week, the unions were able to disperse the following sums:

Union	Number relieved	Paid to each
Power Loom Weavers	7,894 weavers	4s.
	127 weavers	3s.
	847 warpers and winders	4s.
	39 winders	3s.
	226 twisters	4s.
	47 dressers	4s.
	3 handmill warpers	4s.
	894 helpers	2s.
	31 helpers	1s.
Spinners and Self-Actor Minders	841 spinners and minders	7s.

Union	Number relieved	Paid to each
	993 piecers	3s. 6d.
	897 bobbiners	2s.
Card Room Hands	1,335 hands	3s.
	21 hands	2s. 9d.
	17 hands	2s. 6d.
	207 hands	2s. 3d.
	290 hands	2s.
	16 hands	1s. 9d.
	10 hands	1s. 6d.
	25 hands	1s.
Throstle Spinners	381 hands	3s. 3d.
	44 hands	2s.
	22 hands	2s. 9d.
	7 hands	2s. 6d.
	35 hands	1s. 6d.
Tape Machine Sizers	57 hands	8s.
Power Loom Overlookers	181 hands	8s.
	6 hands	7s.
Total	15,720	£2,944 8s. 3d.

Despite this continued flow of strike funds, the distress in the town was all too evident. In December, Giles Howarth, a spokesman for the spinners, suggested that few could imagine the suffering in Preston, unless they were conversant with the 'Homes and haunts of misery'. He told of a Preston family who visited a slaughterhouse regularly, fetched blood and consumed it even without bread to mix with it. Another man was so hungry that he was seen picking bits from wash that had been put by for pigs. As Howarth explained, these were not random statements but the result of observations. He branded the manufacturers of Preston as infamous, for they had driven human beings to such desperation. Yet there were no reports of a significant drift back to work and even during Christmas week, rather than submit to the masters, some twenty spinners and their families moved from Preston to seek work elsewhere. At the same time, almost a hundred other individuals had been removed from the town by the Poor Law officials. At Christmas, the weavers' committee announced a gift of sixpence each to 2,120 of the town's children.

New Year 1854 brought no sign of a breakthrough in the dispute. There was stalemate, but news of the lockout had spread to distant shores. In America, the *Boston Daily Commonwealth* published a report headed 'The white slaves of England', and urged its readers to provide aid and provisions for the Preston workpeople. On 19 January 1854, at another mass meeting of the Preston operatives at the Orchard, it was announced that a benefit evening would take place at the Drury Lane Theatre, London on behalf of the Preston operatives. Sympathy for the town's unemployed was being expressed far and wide.

Later in January, Mr Hollins, proprietor of the Royal Sovereign mill on London Road, announced that he was prepared to ignore the lockout and began trying to tempt his hands back to work, but only offered rates 10 per cent *below* those he had paid prior to the closure of his mill. Only a handful of weavers responded to this offer, but the news that even a small number of operatives had abandoned the struggle led to confrontation. A crowd of strikers gathered outside Hollins' mill and as some of the employees left work, a woman and young lad were apprehended for shouting 'knobstick'. Similar incidents occurred in early February, as a trickle of operatives returned to work. Thomas Bannister of Aqueduct Street appeared in court, charged with smashing the window of a neighbour's house after the neighbour had returned to work at Brookhouse mill. Bannister was convicted and bound over to keep the peace for twelve months. The same week, an elderly Irishwoman named Mary Flanagan was arrested near the Hollins mill for shouting 'knobstick': she admitted the offence and was let off with a caution.

By now the strike committee desperately required an amicable settlement. Arrests and cases of victimisation grew in number. Thus, an employee of one of the leading manufacturers in Preston, Horrocks, Miller & Co., was dismissed after 48 years' continuous service, because he would not compel his daughters to return to work at the reduced wages on offer. In another case, several tenants of the millowner, Ainsworth, had been required as a condition of employment to rent properties in Cotton Court and Back Dale Street. During the lock out, some had accumulated substantial rent arrears and, according to a union official, Waddington, had received an ultimatum from the millowner to pay up or resume work. Waddington protested that these properties were worse than stables or shippons and nobody had the right to expect people to live in such appalling places. But while the union position looked less certain, solidarity on the part of the employers was also weaker. Greatrix & Co., owners of Steam Mill, Fylde Road, conceded the 10 per cent; Rodgett agreed to equalise his rates with those paid at Stockport; and Mr Almond reached a satisfactory deal with his workers. By the middle of February 1854 some 21 local employers were paying rates agreeable to all parties, although 32 mills were still out of action.

At a meeting on 21 February, union officials revealed that the employers were considering importing strikebreakers from other areas, perhaps even the Continent, to end the dispute. Luke Wood, a visiting delegate from Stockport, claimed that the Preston masters had been sending representatives to Scotland and elsewhere to recruit people to work in Preston mills. The operatives were urged to remain peaceful and to respect property and the law, but Gregson, the man who had been dismissed after 48 years, explained to the crowd how he had been sacked simply because he refused to persuade his daughters to 'knobstick'. He had told his employer that if wages were increased, his daughters were ready and willing to work, but the response from his master was dismissal. Another incident was mentioned: a man with ten children was offered 25s. to return to work. After seeking advice from his father, who told him to refuse the money, the man had enlisted in the 34th Regiment rather than submit.

During the last days of February, 62 strikebreakers arrived by train from Manchester. Described by the union delegates as poor creatures who had been misled over the circumstances in Preston, these people had been promised six shillings per week while learning to weave, rising to 15s. when they were proficient. The union had learned in advance that they were coming – the strikebreakers were escorted to the Farmers Arms, near the Orchard, given food and drink and enough money to return to Manchester, and that evening 54 of them left town, amid much cheering at the railway station.

CHAPTER EIGHT

Strikebreakers

THE SUCCESS of the unions in foiling the first attempt to import strikebreakers to the town was short-lived, and brought retaliatory action by the authorities. On 1 March 1854 placards were posted about town, banning groups from congregating on streets or outside cotton mills, under penalty of fines or imprisonment. Ignoring this threat, on 3 March a crowd of 2–3,000 operatives assembled outside the Maudland railway station yard, for the unions had learned that a train carrying Irish strikebreakers was expected. Detachments of police and firemen were present, to maintain order. The train arrived at the station at about 12.45 p.m. and some 45 minutes later the mayor, town clerk and magistrates' clerk turned up. The Riot Act was read and then the police forcibly cleared a path so that the Irish could be conveyed from the station. No serious trouble occurred and the Irish workers were eventually transferred to the Hanover Street mill of Birley Brothers, near North Road. The Irish, numbering about fifty, had travelled from Ulster, via Fleetwood, and some were said to be former inmates of the Belfast workhouse. The *Preston Guardian* reported this development, commenting how

> These people presented a most melancholy sight, nearly all were destitute of shoes and stockings and some were dressed in nightcaps. They included all ages, from the infant in arms to females advanced in years, altogether a wretched specimen of what Irish famine had reduced the peasantry of that Country to.

The same evening, another train arrived in Preston from Warrington, carrying some twenty strikebreakers, who were immediately transferred to the mill of Swainson & Birley at Fishwick. Shortly afterwards, a second batch of Irish from Belfast was hastily escorted to their allocated mills, where it was also intended to house them. Some local operatives reacted bitterly to what they perceived as deliberate provocation by the masters, resulting in a number of arrests. Two youths, Dennis Woodhead and Patrick Bennett, were charged with rioting after a violent incident involving strikebreakers, many of them children, who had come from the north by rail and were being transferred to John and Adam Leigh's mill in Old Lancaster Lane. In Aqueduct Street a large crowd began stoning the carriages carrying the newcomers. The police escort, unable to cope with the situation, sent for reinforcements, but these, too, were greeted with a barrage of missiles. Windows were smashed at Leigh Brothers' mill and there Woodhead and Bennett were apprehended.

Alarmed at the possible consequences of this upsurge in violence, the strike committee called an emergency meeting and urged the operatives to keep the peace and not, in the words of one official, to 'Promote any provocation that could result in scenes of blood'. Such was the prospect of unrest in Preston that the Watch Committee telegraphed the home secretary, requesting that one hundred police officers should be sent to the town immediately. The 34th Regiment, some of whom were local men, were transferred to Sheffield to be replaced by the thousand-strong 77th Regiment, which had journeyed down from Glasgow. A further order by the magistrates, on 4 March 1854, banned all public meetings within the town boundaries, allegedly because of inflammatory language used by union officials at previous meetings. This was a severe blow to the strike committee, for it deprived them of the means of transmitting news and information to the operatives in dispute. A meeting of the hands was hurriedly arranged at Ashton Marsh, on the outskirts of town. As thousands of strikers assembled there, placards were posted informing them that all trespassers would be prosecuted. Fortunately for the union, a farmer called Sharples, who owned land in nearby Cottam, offered the use of a field for the meeting. The union official, Edward Swindlehurst, announced a new phase of the dispute, in which the workers were prohibited from meeting in their own town to discuss grievances. Furthermore, he said, referring to the Crimean War which had recently broken out, 'Whilst hundreds and thousands of our fellow creatures were leaving the shores of England to fight against an obvious despotism, we were harbouring the greatest despot in Europe, the greatest despot in the world.'

The following day, 5 March, another mass meeting was held at Cottam on the land of Mr Thompson, a farmer sympathetic to the Preston operatives. Despite the long walk to the field, 20–30,000 people were estimated to have attended, together with union delegates from other towns. As well as hearing the usual speeches of encouragement, the audience was asked to show pity, rather than hatred or anger, towards the poor Irish immigrants now arriving in Preston. One delegate, Mr Schofield from Stalybridge, captured this theme remarkably well:

When we come to cast a glance over the history of that unhappy country, oh, if we read that history fairly and impartially, it almost makes us weep tears of blood. If ever there were sympathies and feelings, which needed rousing, it was in favour of those poor souls who have come here to supplant you. Fellow men, fellow working men, injure not a hair on their heads, respect them, for their God is our God, they are the same human family, of the same class with ourselves. They are suffering under the iron rod of oppression and that has driven them to seek assistance here. Hurt them not, treat them well, speak to them with kindness, and reason with them in charity. Do this and Ireland, down trodden, insulted, long oppressed Ireland will abandon those feelings of animosity, with which she has been taught to look upon the Saxon race.

To capitalise on the solidarity still being displayed by the Preston operatives, a huge rally at Hoghton, halfway between Preston and Blackburn, was arranged for the weekend of 11–12 March. Enormous crowds assembled on the Saturday, having made the journey by foot. Bands played, banners were unfurled, and thousands of Blackburn operatives arrived after the mills there had shut down at 2 p.m. The following day even greater numbers were present, again including many from Blackburn, and accounts spoke of 50–100,000 people. A special train from Preston, organised by the East Lancashire Railway Company, conveyed almost a thousand people to Hoghton station. It was reported that all the roads around Hoghton were teeming with people throughout the day. The proceedings opened with the singing of the operatives' hymn, 'Assembled beneath the broad blue sky, To thee O God, thy children cry'. On 13 March another 35 Irish people destined for Preston mills arrived from Manchester and awaited collection at Fishergate railway station. As the *Guardian* correspondent observed,

This pitiful looking group of individuals presented the most desperate of sights. These miserable looking specimens of humanity arrived in a most disgustingly filthy condition. Their bedding, etc., swarmed with that species of loathsome vermin so obnoxious to cleanly housewives and when their articles were removed from the truck on which they were packed, the lively insects dispersed themselves over the platform much to the alarm of persons present. A copious supply of boiling water was put in requisition.

With the Preston dispute continuing to attract national attention, a deputation from the Preston Operatives Association managed to secure a meeting with Lord Palmerston, the home secretary. A delegation comprising John Sergeant, George Eccles, Thomas Banks, John Bowman and Edward Whittle spent over two hours at Palmerston's private residence and explained their view of the dispute. Despite listening attentively to their grievances and appearing to take a genuine interest in the proceedings, Palmerston rejected their plea for arbitration. But on Monday 20 March 1854, five of the principal trade unionists were arrested. In a carefully planned operation carried out by the police, George Cowell was detained as he was about to board a train to Manchester and taken to the police station. Mortimer Grimshaw was picked up in Orchard Street at the same time, while James Waddington was seized in his own home. Shortly afterwards, William Parkinson and Thomas Gregson were in custody, while another prominent union man, John Lang, was apprehended the morning after at the Farmers Arms. Shortly afterwards, five more union leaders, Michael Gallaher, Luke Wood, John Brocklehurst, Josiah Dolphin and John Gardner, were arrested. The news spread quickly and soon large groups of workers gathered to await developments. With many of the strike committee now in custody, the remaining activists met in emergency session, which carried on through the night, and on the morning of 21 March a statement was posted throughout the town:

> Whereas our leaders have been apprehended by the Magistrates upon a charge not yet known, we adjure you most earnestly that as you value the cause for which you have so long and so nobly fought, you will keep the peace and not suffer the excitement of the moment to betray you into the slightest offence against the law. To create a disturbance is all that is wanted, for the soldiers are prepared to shoot you down in the streets. There is a law in England greater and wiser than that of the Preston Magistrates and we willingly entrust ourselves and our rights to that law.

That morning, too, the eleven men were transferred from the police lockup to the town hall, amid cries of support and encouragement from the operatives who lined the route. A large crowd gathered outside the town hall and in a packed courtroom, the charges against the men were read out. They were accused of conspiracy, the allegations being 'That they did unlawfully conspire, combine and confederate together and by unlawfully molesting and obstructing certain persons hired by various manufacturers named to work in their trade and business, to force and endeavour to force the said persons so hired, as aforesaid to depart from their said hiring'. These charges related to the events of 27 February, when the Irish strikebreakers were persuaded to return to Manchester. At the hearing, which lasted three days, persistent allegations of intimidation against the strikebreakers were levelled at the defendants. The Preston magistrates committed the accused for trial at Liverpool Assizes. With substantial sureties guaranteed by some local shopkeepers and other sympathisers in the town, bail for the defendants was granted. Immediately after, some tradesmen and others met at the Crown Inn, Church Street, and established a defence fund for which £10 was immediately collected.

News of the arrests was widely reported in the provincial and national newspapers. *The Times*, which had previously been hostile to the operatives' cause, expressed surprise, while the *Manchester Examiner* questioned the wisdom of such extreme measures: 'In all probability, a fresh stimulus will have been given to the weekly subscriptions for the maintenance of the strike and the spirit of antagonism and hostility deepened between the working and capitalist classes.' In contrast, the *Morning Post* felt no sympathy with the Preston eleven and declared that 'The Government has acted wisely in having at length arrested Cowell, Grimshaw and Waddington, the leaders of the Preston movement. There can be no doubt the time has arrived when some steps should be taken to put a stop to this system of combination.'

The arrests did not result in the immediate collapse of the dispute, as many might have anticipated. Many of the recently arrived strikebreakers were not finding life in Preston at all congenial. An Irishwoman, Matilda Taylor, who had been hired in Belfast as a lodging-house keeper for the strikebreakers, claimed she was being forced to undertake mill work and, on refusing, had been sacked. The magistrates, with the woman's permission, ordered her agent to pay her fare back to Belfast. Two Irish youths, John Shevlin and Andrew Riley, who had recently been recruited from Belfast workhouse, found themselves completely destitute. They insisted that they had been recruited by the agents of Birley Brothers with a promise of 5s.–6s. a week while learning mill work, but found that they could not afford the necessities of food, coal, candles or laundry. After applying for a passage home, which had been promised if they did not like the employment, both had been sacked. They also claimed that the new clothes issued to them on arrival in Preston had been stripped from them and their old ones returned. The bench ordered an inquiry into the case, while instructing the relieving officer to provide food and lodgings for them, but the boys intimated that they simply wished to return to Ireland.

The dispute had now lasted 33 weeks, but events elsewhere began to influence the outcome of the struggle. In early April 1854, citing poor trade and the onset of the Crimean War as reasons, the Stockport employers withdrew the 10 per cent wage increase awarded previously. The Blackburn masters introduced short time working, with the equivalent reduction in wages. As a considerable part of the weekly donations for the Preston operatives came from Stockport and Blackburn, much of the strike fund was likely to disappear. Signs of a split in the ranks of the various Preston union committees began to appear. The news from Stockport and Blackburn was so alarming that on Saturday 8 April the Preston Spinners and Self Actors Committee issued a statement which in effect abandoned the 10 per cent demand:

> We, the hand mule spinners and self actor minders of Preston, having ever had a sincere desire to arrive at a speedy, honourable and amicable settlement of existing differences and having adopted every proper means we could think of for that purpose, do agree to take an average of the lists of prices paid in the principal manufacturing districts of Lancashire, as the one at which we are ready and willing to resume our employment.

It was clear that, by agreeing to negotiate on an average of wages, rather than the full 10 per cent, the spinners had dropped their original demands. In Stockport 10,000 workers were on strike again, so they could no longer send any funds to Preston. The Preston weavers, like the spinners, now had grave doubts about sustaining their strike fund. They declared that unless a levy of 7d. per loom could be raised from every working operative throughout the cotton districts, nothing more could be done. The unions learned that mischievous rumours were circulating around the manufacturing districts, announcing that the Preston struggle was over. Subscriptions dropped very rapidly – in the week ending 22 April even Blackburn only subscribed £200 – and the Preston Committee frantically tried to find money from elsewhere. The Rochdale operatives agreed to contribute £80–£100 more per week, and those at Ashton-under-Lyne increased their subscription by £20. Meetings were held in Yorkshire, with workers in Barnsley and Halifax offering support. In just over a week some £1,923 had been promised, including an anonymous donation of £400, but it was not enough.

By 25 April a small number of Horrockses weavers had resumed work at the old terms, and in the last week of April the 410-strong Throstle Spinners Committee agreed to abandon the dispute and return to work on terms dictated by the employers. The amalgamated committee (representing all the unions) was forced to accept that, with the drastic reduction in income, donations to the cardroom hands would have to be cut by two-thirds. There were 1689 cardroom employees, and they would now receive only 1s. per week.

Many of them gave in, and offered themselves for work. Although as yet only 27 of the 815 spinners had resumed work, and although resolve among the weavers remained relatively strong, it is clear that the strike was beginning to crumble.

The Preston Spinners Committee wrote to the employers on 22 April 1854, pleading with them to show compassion and let the men and women return to work with some degree of dignity. The masters, now anticipating complete victory, refused to enter into any negotiations. On 29 April a mass meeting was held on the banks of the Ribble at Walton-le-Dale. George Cowell addressed the operatives and his intensely emotional speech signalled to everyone present that the struggle was almost over:

> There will be no more lockouts, depend on that ... The Preston masters will ever remember the names of Cowell and his compatriots. They will ever remember the Preston operatives of this day and generation. This strike will be handed down to posterity and depend upon it, our children and there children will bless the day when we made such a resolute stand against tyranny and oppression.

He left the platform to loud applause and cheering.

On 1 May, at a mass meeting in the same place, the Preston Power Loom Weavers Association recommended its members to return to work. A series of speakers attacked the tactics of the masters and their supporters but finally the following resolution was proposed: 'That the best thanks of the people of Preston be given to the trades of England, for their magnificent support during this protracted struggle'. The meeting dispersed with resolute cheering for the 10 per cent cause, but with a decision to abandon the strike. Many of the operatives were defiant to the very end, but they knew that many of the people in the town were facing starvation. The subscriptions gathered by 2 May totalled just £1,002, and each weaver received only 2s. 6d. The privations simply could not continue. The decision of the weavers was widely reported, with the *Daily News*, which had consistently condemned the stance of the Preston operatives, stating that 'There is something noble in the self-sacrifice, which has been exhibited by these thousands. They have submitted quietly and resignedly to privations without the slightest attempt to revenge themselves on those, whom they rightly or wrongly, considered as the authors of evil.'

Learning of the decision of the weavers earlier in the day, the Spinners and Self Actors Committee arranged an urgent meeting in the Albion Inn. They faced an acute dilemma, for with the majority of weavers and ancillary trades returning to work, leaving the cotton masters in a position to dictate terms, the spinners might not even be able to maintain pre-lockout rates. There was heated debate, and eventually it was resolved that 'We the Spinners and Self Actors of Preston do hereby pledge ourselves not to resume work until we gain our objective. That is, the same prices we had previous to being locked out or an average of the trade.' With no firm commitment from the employers concerning wage rates, the spinners remained defiant, but for the great majority of cotton workers the lockout was over. As the mills reopened, some of them after 38 long weeks, thousands of men, women, and children reported for work once again. Cotton production, as vital to the people of Preston as the very air they breathed, yet often the source of so much discontent, could resume. The dominance of the cotton masters had been threatened, but yet again they had emerged victorious. As *The Times* reported, 'All that is shown by the present conclusion is that in these trials of endurance, capital is usually stronger than labour'. Even so, after 1854 the town's employers would never again collectively test the resolve of their workforces for such a protracted period.

On the general return to work, three of the employers who had awarded the full 10 per cent rise at the start of the dispute decided to withdraw these rates. At the mills of Napier and Goodair, Gardner, and Dawson, notice was given that a fortnight from following the resumption of work, the rates in force prior to October 1853 would apply. There were indications that the spinning masters intended to import more strikebreakers from Glasgow, to break the spinners' continuing action. On 8 May Thomas Banks, secretary of the spinners' union, pleaded with the employers to resume negotiations. The reply he received left the spinners in no doubt about the intentions of the Preston Committee of the Masters Association: 'a considerable number of spinners and piecers have already resumed work and [we] can only recommend those still wishful for employment to seek for any information they require at the respective mills'. While the spinners remained in dispute, some 2–3,000 weavers had no work, because the supply of yarn was not back to normal, and a large number of cardroom hands were also idle. After nine months of mass unemployment and extreme privation, the suffering of the townspeople was not yet over. Even after the return to work, more than 260 additional applications for relief were made to the Preston Board of Guardians. A reconciliation committee was organised, to urge the spinners to end their dispute. A petition signed by almost 400 shopkeepers and independent tradesmen was presented to the spinners, stating that further resistance was futile, while the spinners were reminded of the increasing financial burden upon the town because of the mounting distress.

On the evening of Sunday 14 May the Preston Spinners and Self Actors Committee held another meeting, to consider a recommendation passed by a delegate conference held in Manchester earlier in the day to the effect that the Preston spinners, in order to prevent any further suffering, should call off the strike. The spinners faced a tough decision, for their principled stance not only created suffering in Preston but also conflicted with most public opinion. One delegate referred to a recent incident, when he had witnessed a poor weaver begging for a shilling to purchase straw, on which he could rest himself and his family. Another delegate insisted that the spinners might be retreating but were not beaten. He hoped, now that the most trying time had come, that they would conduct themselves with manliness and dignity. A delegate who had made the journey from London praised the Preston spinners, saying that 'He had heard so much about Preston people and now he had beheld them for himself. They had convinced the Country of the justice of their claim and would be able again to awaken its sympathy when they required it.' There was little choice. The resolution to return to work was agreed. The final discussion concerned the fate of the strikers when they went back, for it was reported that some 700 employers in the industry had decided that no trade union activist should be employed in future. Thanks were given for the tremendous support from the public and other trades throughout the nation, and in a final act of defiance, the spinners decided to meet together at 7 a.m. the following day and march proudly to their respective mills.

The most controversial and damaging trade dispute ever witnessed in Britain was over. On Monday 15 May 1854, 785 spinners, 1,196 piecers and 805 bobbiners offered themselves for employment, bringing full production back to Preston's mills. In the same week, the powerloom weavers released a statement which concluded:

once more we summons you to the watchtowers of right and justice. The Preston movement failed, but their cause was just. Let us profit by the example of the spider and persevere until we conquer. If one plan fails, another must be tried. If strikes won't do, let's give them up and raise the flag of emigration and co-operation, the two great levers which are destined to raze the strongholds of tyranny and oppression to the earth, and erect upon their ruins a monument of the people's rights which shall make them independent and self employed.

Shortly after the great Preston lockout ended, *The Leader* published a report on the dispute:

Associated masters of Preston, condescend to learn a lesson from the past and improve the tone of feeling between your workpeople and yourselves. Learn that they are not your menial servants, but your helpmates. Learn to respect their rights and they will learn to respect you. Strive to improve their condition, socially and mentally and in doing so you cannot fail to better yourselves in both respects. Above all if you must have a victory, conquer your prejudices, conquer your pride, conquer your avarice. These will be victories indeed.

At the Liverpool Assizes in August 1854, the eleven union activists faced charges of conspiracy. The judge said he was extremely pleased that the Preston dispute had terminated, for had the defendants been tried and found guilty, he should have felt it his duty to pass upon them a severe sentence. He hoped the risk they had each run would be a warning to them not to engage in such activity again. By industry, said the judge, they might become masters themselves. He hoped they would go home and strive to maintain their families in comfort and respectability and that such lamentable disputes would never happen again. The eleven were discharged forthwith, but for George Cowell a further ordeal had to be endured. In November 1854, he was incarcerated in the debtors' gaol at Lancaster castle. When the Preston strike had ended the unions were heavily in debt, in particular with printing bills, and could not repay them. As a result, Cowell was arrested and imprisoned. An appeal to the Preston operatives was issued, with workplace and street collections organised, until finally, George Cowell was released.

CHAPTER NINE

The Cotton Famine

B Y THE END OF 1861, men were slaughtering one another in their thousands during the American Civil War, and the economic impact of the war was being felt in Lancashire. The blockade of the Southern States by the Union navy, designed to wreck the economy of the breakaway Confederacy, was constricting the supplies of raw cotton to the textile industries of the Old World. Three-quarters of the cotton used by the Lancashire manufacturers came from the southern United States, and it was inevitable that problems would soon develop. Contrary to widespread belief, then and now, the blockade, and the major reduction in supplies of raw materials, was not the only cause of the economic difficulties which Lancashire faced. Recent analysis by economic historians has demonstrated that during the late 1850s and the first two years of the 1860s the manufacturers of cotton cloth in Lancashire had grossly over-produced. The domestic market was saturated, and firms were stockpiling unsold cloth and yarn for which no outlet could be found. This over-production meant that a cutback was almost unavoidable and, largely by accident, this happened to coincide with the outbreak of large-scale war on the other side of the Atlantic.

In Preston there had been an apparent boom since the end of the great lockout in the spring of 1854. The population of the town had grown rapidly, reaching almost 83,000 in 1861, and no fewer than fifteen new cotton mills had been opened in the eight years from the end of the lockout. For the producers and manufacturers, at least, this had been a time for expansion and increased profitability. For ordinary workers the housing and sanitary conditions of the town continued to worsen, however. When a correspondent from the *The Builder* toured Preston in 1861 he saw appalling conditions, which he described graphically:

> Rows of houses building, with old brick bats taken out of rubbish heaps, on the unhealthy plan of digging a pit in the earth for a kitchen. Others in Spring Row, already built with pigsties, pits and water butts on higher

Kirkham Street, photographed around 1935, looking towards Fylde Road. This street, with families living in cellars, was described vividly by the correspondent of *The Builder* during 1861.

ground behind them, so that all overflowing and percolations behind them must filter through the houses, the floors of which are below the level of the soil in the rear. Common privies in front of the houses, muddy coal ash roads and clothes hanging out to dry ... Will this generation never learn the absurdity of placing floors below the level of the surrounding soil and then of placing water butts, privies and pigsties close to them with no drainage. How long will Doctors come and go and cure fever, rheumatism and other ills and the causes of them not to be removed.

Moving on to the Fylde Road and Aqueduct Street area, he noted that:

By the side of the Aqueduct Inn is another one of those unaccountable pieces of mismanagement we have noticed before. The end of a sewer discharges the whole of what drainage there is upon the face of the land. A vacant piece of ground is here bounded on three sides by the rear out buildings of houses and on the fourth side this sewage forms a stream. The space within it is used as a playground for children. A butcher close by makes use of this space in which to bury a few inches beneath the surface, the blood, guts, and offal from his slaughterhouse. Another similar space is left further off Fylde Road, were a sort of crater in the centre is full of stagnant slime. There are back to back houses with cruelly small yards all of which have privies and pits with two holes made in the wall at the end of the row for the overflowings to be carried to the rest of the sewage streamlets, with which this neighbourhood is defiled.

Of the Maudland area, one of the worst parts of the town, he recorded that

There contracted yards and crowded ash pits overhang the steep bank of a canal. The view from the canal bridge is ghastly. There are a few wretched decayed trees on the banks and the overhanging privies and dung middens have discharged their surplus filth into the canal and the water has the appearance of a stagnant sheet of fluid with a thick oleaginous brown crust on it. In the neighbourhood of the celebrated Horrocks factory is Kirkham Street, were families live in horrible cellars, a second family above them on the ground floor and a third over that. The roads are made of coal ash, the yards so confined that the people must hang out their clothes to dry in the street, at the doors, on the stairs, over the beds, or else over the terrible choked offal pits that are within a pace of the back doors. Moss Street is occupied on one side by a factory, on the other by a row of back to back houses for the operatives. As there are no yards, there are no privies for the whole accommodation of the whole colony of families who live in the cellars and first and second floors. There are privies built at the end of the street and the occupants of the other end of the street must traverse the whole length of it, not only to use them, but to dispose of all their refuse.

The correspondent recorded one final observation:

With better health and a better education, other careers would open up for the Preston operatives, who now have but the choice of entering the factory or the army. The enlisting sergeant will tell you that there are more recruits

Hill Street, off Friargate, looking east, *c.*1949. From photographs such as these one can gain a good impression of how cramped and insanitary such areas were, particularly in the era before proper or adequate water supply and sewerage. It was in these narrow streets and passageways in 1862 that typhus first appeared.

to be had in Preston than in any other town in the Kingdom, but they are so weak with there tea and bread diet, that it takes two years to feed them up to be soldiers. Under there present conditions, the men of Preston are old at forty, at forty-five they are old and done. If our well meant words have any effect, the rising generation may last a little longer.

By October 1861, the cotton trade throughout Lancashire was experiencing considerable difficulties. At least a dozen of Preston mills were reduced to four day working, and seven others operated a three-day week. At the end of October, it was announced that the mills belonging to the Leigh Brothers, Ainsworth's and James Naylor would have to close within a month. The cotton masters association had already informed operatives that a 7½ per cent reduction in wages was necessary to carry them through the current crisis. Real hardship was immediately evident in Preston: the number of inmates in the workhouse in mid-November was 747, compared 531 in the corresponding period in 1860. As the distress grew, a committee was established to seek ways of alleviating the hardship. It was decided that the able-bodied unemployed should be put to work at various tasks for one shilling per day. Stone-breaking was authorised, as was excavation and levelling work on Preston Moor, a large tract of Corporation-owned land on the northern edge of the town. Stone-breaking was a particularly effective method of providing relief as stone purchased at 3s. per ton could, after breaking, be sold as gravel at 4s. per ton. Plans were drawn up to bring in substantial amounts from north Lancashire by canal, and the Ribble Navigation Company was asked to dredge the river to provide a further supply. The latter would be used as gravel to repair the town's streets.

Unemployment continued to rise and the Preston Spinners Union accused the masters of gross mismanagement prior to the crisis, accusing them of speculation and lowering the price of yarn by over-production. More measures were proposed to alleviate the poverty of the unemployed. In late November 1861 it was suggested that they should labour on the construction of a large main sewer to serve the new St Georges Road, linking Deepdale Road to St Paul's Road. It was expected that over one hundred labourers would be put in this work during the forthcoming winter. The poverty generated other forms of discontent. Several spinners and piecers at William Taylor's Old Tulketh mill near Fylde Road withdrew their labour without notice. Despite accusations from the strikers of failing to pay agreed piecework rates, Taylor appealed to the Board of Guardians for a number of unemployed spinners to be made available to him. Other sporadic strikes occurred in Preston, but the general opinion of the unions was that organised resistance to the wage cuts during the current climate was futile. At the end of November 1861, they grudgingly accepted the 7½ per cent reduction, although criticising the millowners:

Capital knows no law but one, that of self-interest. We did think there were a few honourable employers, who would on this occasion set the others an example by not enforcing the reduction. But vain hope, the last plank that we cling to has been shattered, the veto has gone forth. Shylock has demanded his pound of flesh.

During December William Bashall's Wellfield Road mill joined those which had completely stopped, but the Brookfield Street mill of Napier and Goodair, Dawson's Mill on Fylde Road, and Dixon's off Heatley Street, returned to full time working. Other establishments were still on a three or four day weeks. During this confused period, the unions unsuccessfully lobbied the manufacturers to equalise the amount of raw cotton available, and thereby pull everyone through the crisis. In the early weeks of 1862 there was another round of devastating mill closures, including Rodgett's in Bow Lane, Eastham's at Fishwick, and Walker Brothers off Grimshaw Street.

In mid-December soup kitchens were opened, and in just five days some 3,260 quarts of soup were sold, at one penny per portion, to the poor of the town. On Christmas Eve, the Board of Guardians announced that the number of inmates in local workhouses was 899, while during the first week of January 1862 some 6,000 were receiving out relief (that is, they remained in their own homes). About 100 men were employed in stone-breaking and stone-gathering and some 500 were at work on Preston Moor. The mortality statistics for the last quarter of 1861 highlighted the grimness of the task faced. There were 655 deaths in that period, an increase of 153 on the corresponding quarter of 1860. In late January committees for the collection of subscriptions, relief distribution and visiting the poor were organised and the opening of additional soup dispensaries, and the distribution of bread and coal, were arranged. The main soup kitchen in Upper Walker Street was in such demand, that every Monday morning large groups of people congregated outside waiting to be admitted. Many of these unfortunates had eaten nothing the previous day when the kitchen was closed. The additional soup kitchens promised by the authorities opened at the beginning of February 1862, the one situated near the Three Tuns public house on North Road dispensing 2,921 quarts in a week. A local provision dealer, Mr Christopher Hargreaves of Lancaster Road, undertook to distribute pea soup at one penny per quart from his premises.

In the first week of March the official soup kitchens distributed no less than 18,486 quarts of soup, and the relief fund itself was under severe stress.

The first month of 1862 saw a major deterioration in an already bad situation. By the end of January over 850 men had been put to work on the Moor, and 1003 people were in the workhouse. Figures published by the Preston Spinners and Self Actors Committee towards the end of January reveal the level of unemployment and short time working:

Working full time	30 mills	11,390 operatives
Working 5-day week	2 mills	741 operatives
Working 4-day week	10 mills	3,047 operatives
Working 3½-day week	2 mills	945 operatives
Working 3-day week	9 mills	6,375 operatives
Stopped entirely	17 mills	4,046 operatives
Total	**70 mills**	**26,544 operatives**

The public relief fund was now operating and those operatives in work responded with compassion, trying to help their fellows who were unemployed and suffering great distress. The workers at Lancaster and Isherwood's mill donated £26 6s., while those at Gardner' Kay Street mill offered to give a weekly donation to the fund as long as required. Begging had become an acute problem, one which the authorities found difficult to tackle. A local man, charged with begging in Berry and Knowsley Streets in the Avenham district, was found to be a self-actor minder previously employed at Sharples and Wildings mill in Fletcher Road, and to have resorted to begging because he had no change of clothes and hoped to procure a shirt. A considerable amount of bread was being given to the most destitute: during a six-day period in early March 1862 the following numbers of loaves were distributed:

St John's Ward	697
St Peter's Ward	2,353
Fishwick Ward	556
Christ Church Ward	392
St George's Ward	1,580
Trinity Ward	1,546
Total	**7,124**

Applications for soup were administered by tickets given to the most desperate, or by sale at one penny per quart or a halfpenny per basin,

National attention was brought to the plight of the Lancashire cotton operatives during the Cotton Famine in engravings such as this, which appeared in the *Illustrated London News* in 1863.

for those still able to earn some sort of income. The presence of so many destitute people queuing for soup presented a most pitiful sight, as the *Preston Guardian* commented: 'We would recommend Ladies and Gentlemen residing at the west end occasionally to slip down to the soup establishment. It would convince them that the saying, one half of a world does not know how the other half lives is no fiction.' Other steps on behalf of the poor were undertaken, including the formation of a Ladies Committee which offered various forms of assistance. Many of the sick poor were referred to these ladies, who would provide them with beef tea, barley gruel and other nutritious food. At premises in Lord Street, a workroom was set up where destitute young women and girls undertook sewing, knitting, and mending in return for the relief they were receiving.

On 9 April 1862 the largest of the town's firms, Horrocks, Miller & Co., declared that production at the majority of their mills would be restricted to a four-day week. Some 150 men were now breaking stone at Leighton Street and about 1,050 working on the moor or beside the river, while thousands more receiving other forms of help. Five days later, Lord Shaftesbury spoke in the House of Lords about the plight of the distressed areas of Lancashire. In response, the Government appointed a Poor Law inspector, Henry Farnall, to assess the situation. He arrived in Preston on 14 May and began his tour of the town, visiting the stone yard, the land known as the Moor and elsewhere. He was deeply moved by the plight of the poor and, reporting on work at the stone yard, said that 'Nearly all their hands were so blistered that they could not close them after dropping their hammers. It was impossible to expect them to go on with such work.' Of the men toiling at the moor, he thought that the relief given to them was scarcely sufficient to maintain muscular strength. But he was clear that the ratepayers of Preston would have to bear the financial burden of assistance, and the government would contribute nothing. Farnall stated that 'No ratepayer of Preston, however commercial he may be, will desire this state of things to last. The people have a right to live, they must be fed. Poverty is not a crime to be punished by starvation', but Preston would pay. The *Preston Guardian* echoed this view, commenting that 'Three shillings rate should be sufficient to take us over this distress we may anticipate between this and next December'.

The ripples spread. By late May 1862 local banks were said to be exhausted for funds, as almost £17,500 in savings, put aside for a rainy day, had been withdrawn by workers from their accounts. The Trade unions had donated over £700 to impoverished members and families, and charitable donations had exceeded £9,000, but many ordinary folk had been forced to pawn all their goods, and thousands were absolutely destitute. At the end of May 1862, figures on the number of unemployed in the town were published in the *Preston Guardian*:

Trade	Unemployed	Average weekly wage when at work
weavers	6,004	10s.
winders, warpers, tapers, dressers	1,441	12
cardroom hands	1,421	10s.
spinners, self-actor minders, piecers and creelers	1,615	19s. [spinners]
throstle hands	250	not known
Total	10,371	

THE LANCASHIRE DISTRESS.—THE SOUP-KITCHEN, CROOKED-LANE, PRESTON.

These figures accounted for nearly half the estimated 23,500 operatives normally employed in Preston mills, but many more were on short-time working. In all 16,772 people, including 540 at the sick room in Lord Street, were registered as receiving relief. For many of the townspeople, the meagre diet of bread and soup issued by the relief committee was the only means of sustenance. Their demeanour was noted by the *Preston Guardian* on 12 July 1862: 'The same painful monotony of deepening wretchedness, borne with the same quiet fortitude which for so long a period has claimed the sympathy and won the admiration of all classes. Following Farnall's visit to Preston in May, the lord mayor of London introduced a special fund for the Lancashire operatives, as awareness of the level of suffering spread across the country, while in Preston, the soldiers garrisoned at Fulwood contributed the sum of £13 to the relief fund.

For some unfortunates in the town, the hopelessness of the situation was simply too much to bear. In December 1861 a poor woman called Pedder, living in Walkers Court, off Friargate, attempted suicide by hanging but was discovered by neighbours, who immediately summoned a policeman. The officer described the house as the most miserable and squalid abode he ever saw. The husband, wife and six small children were in the very lowest depths of poverty: none of them had tasted food that day, and the children were lying on the bare flags with not even any straw or a rag to cover them. Tea and provisions were made available to enable them to get through the night and, after applying for relief the following day, the whole family was admitted to the workhouse. Early in July 1862, a man named Warren, who lived with his wife and children in a cellar in Moss Street, off Fylde Road, attempted suicide by slitting his throat. His plight had become so desperate that he had applied to the Board of Guardians for relief. He received an order to be admitted to Ribchester workhouse some miles away, while his wife and children were to be taken to Preston workhouse. The poor man was so depressed at his situation and forthcoming separation from his family, that his life no longer seemed tolerable. Rescued in time, he was taken to the House of Recovery. Churches of all denominations throughout the land appealed for donations for the impoverished operatives. In its issue of 9 July 1862 *The Nonconformist* revealed how such subscriptions were put to good use. It used the example of donations of 2s. 3d. 'for a dinner of a poor family' given by Ada and 2s. 6d. from Nelly:

> I just learn that Nelly's half crown is to give a nice suet dumpling, some meat to make some broth and a loaf for seven little children whose Mother is very ill and whose Father earned one shilling and sixpence last week and for weeks before nothing. The house is the cleanest in the district. Ada's two shillings and threepence will give a dinner of soup and meat tomorrow to five little children whose Mother is dying and also a loaf to three more whose Mother is ill and the little girl of six has to do all the housework. Surely the dear little girls will be pleased to know this.

Among the men toiling away at Preston Moor, signs of dissent appeared in November 1862 when proposals were submitted to subject the workers to military-style marching and drilling exercises. This idea was suggested by the Board of Guardians to promote the physical welfare of the men, as well as for disciplinary purposes. The men were angered by this demand, and the apparent implication that that they were 'idlers', and categorically refused to participate in the humiliating of drilling. The reluctance of the Guardians to adjust the daily working hours, so that the men could purchase food before the majority of shops closed, also fuelled the sense of resentment.

The majesty of its architecture could not disguise the suffering to be found within its walls: the Preston Union workhouse which was built in the 1860s, well away from the town centre, on Watling Street Road.

PHOTOGRAPH: CARNEGIE, 2007

But if Prestonians thought the situation could not deteriorate further, they were mistaken. Sporadic cases of fever were reported, and Dr Buchanan, from the medical department of the Privy Council, inspected the town in November 1862. Typhus had broken out. Buchanan concluded that a combination of poor diet, overcrowding, insufficient clothing and inadequate bedding contributed to the transmission of the disease. He urged that more relief be administered and overcrowding prevented, and the town clerk explained that the homes of the poor were being lime-washed and overcrowding dealt with. Typhus first appeared in the Canal Street and Hope Street area at the northern end of Friargate, with other cases in nearby Foster's Square and Vicar Street off Walker Street. The inadequate drainage systems and filthy alleyways, common in these districts, were thought to encourage the disease. In November 1862 Farnall, the official who had previously visited the town, claimed that the degree of pauperism in Preston was 7 per cent above the average of 27 other blighted cotton towns. Some 16,619 people, 20 per cent of the population, were

Terraced housing in Preston, used to illustrate Revd Clay's report, 1840s. Each house has a small back yard with a privy, and the narrow gap acts as an open sewer. Proper sewers were not built in working-class areas in Preston until well after the disease epidemics of the mid-nineteenth century.

being relieved by the Board of Guardians. The operative classes were not alone in being badly affected by the crisis. One shopkeeper admitted in January 1863 that 'For many a day together, they do not take a single halfpenny', and another said in the week before Christmas 1862 that he 'took only eightpence'. Many others were reported to be on the brink of ruin.

Grave concern was now expressed over the welfare of the womenfolk, especially the young, who were regarded as extremely vulnerable. The charitable organisations began to arrange home visits and in November a *Preston Guardian* correspondent visited some homes in St Peters ward:

At one house where there were no chairs, no tables or crockery, an empty cupboard and a fireplace which had held neither fuel nor flame for nine months, sat on an old rickety form two fine interesting young women in their honest pride, ashamed of their condition and crouching as much as they could out of sight, for they were half naked. They had neither frock, nor bonnet, nor clogs and the underclothing they wore had to be washed overnight, no change did they possess. Of food they had none and they had neither 'bite nor sup' that day.

The district visitor informed the correspondent that this was no isolated case. As a palliative, some young women were given the opportunity of attending the Knowsley Street School in Avenham, which was financed by charity. With room for over 500 girls of all denominations, it offered training in seamstressing, knitting and other skills, while instruction in reading writing and arithmetic was offered in nearby Shepherd Street. The girls were mainly employed making flannel singlets or knitted stockings for distribution to the poor or the workhouse. Each was expected to contribute a small sum from her one shilling wage each day and eventually to purchase material to make an item of clothing for herself. They were bound by rigid rules:

1. Particular attention is to be observed in attending punctually at the hours appointed;
2. No loud talking or conversation will be permitted;
3. All the females employed in this school are requested to come clean and orderly in their persons and dress;
4. Any female guilty of disobedience, injuring or destroying the articles given to them to work up, or doing anything contrary to these rules, will be discharged and there relief cancelled;
5. Any female who does not conduct herself satisfactorily will have her ticket withdrawn and an order given to her to go into the Workhouse as the Guardians may determine.

On 15 November 1862 the *Preston Guardian* reported on a recent tour of the major soup kitchen and relief centre situated at Crooked Lane, off Lancaster Road. Its correspondent noted the sign displayed by the entrance which said 'You must all come clean', but remarked how the people had more than enough to do in procuring bread, and many could not buy soap. According to the visitor:

For the ones who do not come clean … a huge tub, which is constantly supplied with clean hot water, soap and rough towels is provided. None of the applicants are allowed to take their soup or bread unless clean. There was a couple of ragged urchins, with scarce a shirt to cover their backs and with caps which brightly shone with grease and their sweep like faces were not so easily divested of the deep pitted darkness which covered them. The ceremony of washing over, they scampered to the distributor of soup. Up came a tall gaunt fellow who had to exercise immense care lest, in pulling of his fustian coat, it should become more tattered than it was and when doffed, revealed a shirt with but one sleeve. This man had through dire necessity been compelled to beg his bread. He greatly enjoyed his wash, then off went he in his tattered clothes and shouldering his wallet to pay his halfpenny for his meal of soup.

Continuing his tour, the reporter wrote that

The Avenue leading to the soup dispensers is thronged as early as six in the morning. They present to the ticket collector their card and in line moves the procession, slowly and orderly. The ticket man cries aloud the quantity to be allowed to each person. A posted notice states, be as silent as possible. It is a wonder that a hungry, half starved mass of people like those who frequent the soup kitchen are as orderly as they are. It is a credit to them and another evidence of the patience, endurance and fortitude with which the operatives of Lancashire have borne and are bearing their unparalleled trial.

Several of the operatives spoke to the newspaperman, one saying, 'There's neawt but th' soup between me an' starvation', while another remarked, 'If it wurn't for th' soup, half th' town would ha' been deead long ago'. With the national spotlight firmly fixed on the plight of the northern cotton towns, newspaper reporters from far and wide journeyed to Preston. A correspondent representing the *Leeds Mercury* described his observations after his brief stay in the town:

I visited several Irish families who as a rule kept their rooms cleanly, which rendered the deficiency of clothing and bedding the more observable. It was curious to note the attempts made to render any treasured article, such as a clock or looking glass, which had escaped the general wreck, as conspicuous as possible. Many of the cottages in the older portions of Preston are constructed on very objectionable principles. At first sight it seems incredible that English factory workmen should be compelled to dwell in such places, but such is the fact and I feel almost ashamed to state it. In one of this class of dwellings I found two elderly females, one of whom formerly gained a livelihood by collecting rags and bones. The cellar in which one of these poor creatures slept possessed no fireplace, the window was merely a small glazed aperture and the walls and floor were reeking with damp. The next house was worse still and when I entered the cellar, the absence of fireplace and window rendered it necessary to procure a candle, when a sorry scene presented itself to my view. The bed itself was nothing but an old rotten sack, guiltless of possession of chaff and blessed with simply a thin sheet and tattered counterpane, yet it formed the sleeping place of several factory workers, who bore a good name for industry and steadiness.

The antagonism felt by the men on the Moor had spread to the Leighton Street stone-breaking site, where 130 men struck on 17 December. Previously they were paid a shilling per day to crush stones, but now a piecework system was being proposed, whereby a ton of stone would have to be broken in return for the shilling. Incensed by this, the men occupied the Poor Office in Lancaster Road, some staying overnight. Police were called but the men reiterated their demands that payment by the day should be continued. The Guardians listened to the grievances and agreed to relax the rules, especially in poor weather, and a review was ordered to ascertain what quantity of stone could reasonably be crushed each day. By the beginning of January 1863, the main relief outlet at Crooked Lane was distributing quantities of clothing and bedding for the absolute needy, while coal could also be applied for. Figures published on 3 January showed the numbers in receipt of coal:

Ward	Persons	Coal (tons)
St John's	3,210	59
Christ Church	1,585	25
St Peter's	16,543	228
Fishwick	5,879	89
St George's	5,949	96
Trinity	6,670	103
Total	39,836	600

On 16 January, at a meeting called by the spinners and minders, many operatives expressed anger towards the 'Labour Test'. Examples were given

The smart avenue to the right of this engraving was laid out before Preston industrialised, but the area to the left, Avenham Park, was one of the areas built in order to provide work for unemployed cotton operatives during the Cotton Famine. Just visible is a short section of the horse tramway which connected the Lancaster Canal to a branch of the Leeds and Liverpool Canal at Walton Summit.

CARNEGIE COLLECTION

by men sent by the Board to the new cattle market project in Brook Street. Although only 300 spades were available, over 1200 men were compelled to turn up every day, the majority standing around with no work and therefore no pay. Accusations were made of vindictiveness against known union men in the way work was allocated, as were allegations of favouritism by some on the relief committee. It was said that anyone who had connections with members of the committee was treated favourably, while cases of the most abject poverty were being ignored. Concern was also raised as to why some of the ladies assigned to visit the homes of the poor would inquire about the religion of the occupant before entering.

Now, Dr Buchanan presented his report on the fever epidemic. He stated that 227 cases of typhus had occurred in Preston between midsummer and

November 1862, resulting in almost fifty deaths, and reported a loss of strength, colour and flesh among the operatives who had been visited by the medical men charged with the poorer districts. A visitor, he commented, observed

a wan and haggard look about the people, that he will hear from those who know them is no wise habitual to them. He may see for himself the truth of an observation constantly made by the medical men, that the parents have lost their health much more generally than the children and particularly that the Mothers, who most of all starve themselves have got pale and emaciated. Children have suffered less in strength and robustness.

Diarrhoea was reportedly very prevalent in Preston: 'The disease has been especially intractable. In no other town had any such excess been observed.' Scurvy was reported in Preston as elsewhere in the cotton belt, while the greatest incidence of *purpura* [bleeding into the skin] was in Preston, Blackburn and Stockport. Boils and carbuncles were also a major problem in Preston and Salford.

This comprehensive report emphasised that the unemployed mothers normally gave their infants more care than would hired nursery keepers and, although ignorance and poverty meant that these children could be fed better, they were largely guarded from death by neglect or opium. Urging the local manufacturers to address this problem, Buchanan called for organised nurseries. Establishments of this kind in London were noted as being healthy, well arranged places where children could be maintained and returned in good health to their mothers, at a weekly rate of twopence for an infant or fourpence for a child requiring meat. In contrast, in the cotton towns weekly care often cost 3s., with drugging often inflicted on the infant and high mortality rates reflecting this scandal.

In his summary, Buchanan pulled no punches. Although noting that starvation in the cotton districts was rare, he observed the particularly low state of health, especially among the elderly poor. Scurvy and haemorrhages were frequent while lung disease was disproportionate among the unemployed, even allowing for the season. Epidemic measles and scarlet fever habitually exhibited peculiarities that in ordinary times were only seen in those with weak constitutions. Housing rent was another problem, as many unemployed were using relief money to pay rent, and so had little left for food. Many families had moved in with others, increasing overcrowding and the diseases associated with it. Buchanan urged the local authorities to issue free bath tickets, cleanliness being so vitally important while the distress continued.

Fortunately, by February 1863 the typhus outbreak was on the wane. In every home of a known victim, thorough cleansing, lime-washing and disinfecting was carried out. The bedding was destroyed, and replacements provided by the relief committee. The fever had been predominantly found in a cluster of narrow streets and courts at the northern end of Friargate, although other streets had been affected – Patten Street, Back Newton Street, Leeming Street, Green Street, Great George Street, Sleddon Street and Castle Street in the Moor Lane area had all suffered.

In March 1863 an estimated 14,500 operatives were out of work, and almost 7,000 more on short time. A steady rise in these figures brought the number of completely unemployed in Preston up to 15,000 by April, well over half the cotton workforce. Faced with this continued increase, the Board of Guardians met to consider increasing the working hours for men engaged at the cattle market and on the Moor. It was alleged that some of the men were lazy, and others complained that the working hours were lower than those of normal employment. The men retaliated that the Board of Guardians had shown favouritism in the way tasks were allocated. After two years of unparalleled poverty, with only a subsistence diet, the men also complained that heavy outdoor physical work was becoming unbearable. On 21 April 1863 a confrontation with the Guardians began. An effigy of one of the Guardians was publicly paraded and then buried in a macabre ceremony; men at the cattle market and Moor refused to work; and in the town a mob of up to 8,000 people gathered outside the police station. A delegation of the men met the mayor and the chairman of the Guardians to express their grievances and to recover some unpaid wages due to the men. Little progress was made and the delegation went outside to inform the crowd of the position.

A number of men surged forward, attempting to force entry to the police station, but they were beaten back by the officers. Despite pleas for calm by, among others, Joseph Livesey, the officers were pelted with stones. They retaliated by charging the crowd with their truncheons. Some officers were seriously injured. Eventually the mob dispersed and, fearing further violence, the mayor went from the police station to Fulwood barracks. Shortly after 9 p.m. he returned with 250 foot soldiers. Although the trouble was now over, soldiers remained in the area for an hour before returning to barracks. The following day, three youths (Richard Pye, William Harrison and James Hoyle) were committed for trial for rioting. The situation remained tense. Groups of young men roamed around in a menacing manner and several windows were smashed in Lune Street. As more boisterous youths formed a larger group near the police station in Earl Street, a large body of infantry was spotted marching along Lancaster Road. Under the command of Colonel Hardy, the troops were ordered to fix bayonets and headed for the police station. Large crowds gathered as the military arrived and formed up, and a confrontation seemed likely. As well as the military, every available police officer and fireman had assembled. The mayor refused all requests to meet again with a deputation of the labourers and insisted that if the crowd did not disperse immediately the Riot Act would be read. After a short stand off, the police and firemen burst out of the station with truncheons drawn, moving in various directions and dispersing the mob. Several of the operatives stood their ground but were quickly dealt with by the police, but although some youths and women harried the constables, the mob gradually retreated. By the end of the week, after persistent pleas by the unions to avoid further clashes with the authorities, peace returned to Preston again. Work resumed at the cattle market site and on the Moor, and the Guardians promised that all men working without clogs would shortly be issued with new ones.

Among those witnessing the plight of Preston's poor during the Cotton Famine was the celebrated Lancashire author and commentator Edwin Waugh. He described the case of a poor widow woman with five young children,

driven from house to house by increasing necessity, till they had sunk at last in to a dingy little hovel up a dark court near Hope Street, in one of the poorest parts of the town, where they huddled together about a fireless grate to keep one another warm. In this miserable hole, which I saw afterwards, her husband died of sheer starvation as was declared by the jury on the inquest. The dark damp hovel where they had crept to, was scarcely four yards square and the poor woman pointed to one corner of the floor saying, 'He dee'd i' that nook'. He died there, with nothing to lie upon but the ground and nothing to cover him. His wife and children crept about him there, to watch him die and to keep him warm as best they could.

Waugh recalled a conversation held with one of his local guides, concerning a destitute family:

He found the husband sitting alone in the house, pale and silent. His wife had been brought to bed, two or three days before. 'Hoo's [she's] very ill,' said the husband and after inquiring about the child, the man replied, 'its deeod, it deed yesterday.' He then rose and walked slowly into the next room, returning with a basket in his hands in which the dead child was decently laid out. 'That's o' that's laft on it neaw,' said the poor man. Then, putting the basket upon the floor, he sat down in front of it with his head between his hands, looking silently at the corpse.

Waugh was determined to visit the most deprived areas to see for himself. Entering Walkers Court, off Friargate, he set foot inside a hovel occupied only by a pale crippled woman:

> Her sick head, lapped in a poor white clout, swayed languidly to and fro. Besides being a cripple, she had been ill six years and now her husband was taken ill. He had just crept off to fetch medicine for the two. We did not stop here long; the hand of the ancient master was visible in that pallid face. I think that woman will soon be where the weary are at rest. As we came out, she said slowly and in broken painful utterances, that she hoped the Lord would open the heavens for those who had helped them.

Heartbreaking tales of the most acute misery came to the attention of the author. Accompanied by Mr Toulmin of the relief committee, he called at a house inhabited by an old woman and her only daughter. The daughter had been grievously afflicted with disease of the heart and was quite incapable of helping herself during the last eleven years:

> The poor girl sat panting for breath in the close atmosphere. She sat there in feverish helplessness; sallow and shrunken, unable to bear up her head. I estimated her age to be about twenty-five years. The old widow had just been able to earn what kept body and soul together in her sick girl and herself during the last eleven years, by washing and such like work, but even this resource had fallen away a good deal during these years. Such a life is a good deal like a slow funeral and how true it is that a great many people in this world have only one form of rhetoric for their profoundest experiences, namely, to waste away and die.

Of course, the situation did eventually improve. In June 1863 estimates of the numbers of unemployed suggested a substantial reduction upon the figures of a year earlier. Some 12,559 were totally unemployed, and 27 mills were closed, while almost 24,000 still relied on relief, but this was a significant decrease from the catastrophic level of nearly 40,000 some months previously. The July figures confirmed this trend: the number of mills stopped was down to 22, with 10,922 unemployed. Although the American Civil War continued, the worst really did seem to be over in Preston. Weary of this hardship, some operatives chose to emigrate. The cotton unions were particularly active in obtaining funds to assist such schemes. William Bowes, a former Prestonian who had chosen a new life in America some years previous, wrote to his family still living in the town in a letter published in the *Preston Guardian* on 25 July 1863. He described how he enlisted in the 1st Massachusetts volunteer infantry in August 1862, and went on to say that he was sorry because

> if England or the merchants and shipbuilders of England had not given the so called Confederacy the support they have done, the war would have been ended long ago, but they may give them all the support they can, we will whip them in the end ... I am very badly wounded. I got wounded at the battle of Chancellorville by a rifle bullet. It went through at the end of my ribs, right through my body and came out at my back. I am getting better as well as can be expected. It is seven weeks since I was wounded.

During August and September 1863, unemployment continued to fall, so that by the start of November approximately 10,500 operatives were without work. The reductions were small, but the trend was positive. Yet shocking examples of hardship were still apparent. For example, in September 1863 an unemployed man, John Farington, had managed to obtain work at Gisburn, Yorkshire. There he was joined by his wife, who had been in receipt of relief in Preston but was no longer eligible as her husband was now working. At Gisburn, the woman, who was heavily pregnant, could not find any accommodation – her husband's lodging house was full. They travelled to Blackburn by train and carried on towards Preston on foot. At the Ribble bridge before Brockholes Brow the woman went in to labour and gave birth by the roadside. The gatekeeper of the bridge took the family to his home while a doctor was called but the baby died the following day.

At the end of October, some closed mills reopened with short time working, and the number of unemployed had fallen to 9,739. The signs were hopeful, although (perhaps because of seasonal factors rather than the underlying crisis) during December the position deteriorated once more – by Christmas there were 10,500 unemployed. For the inmates of Preston workhouse, a special Christmas dinner was promised for 88 able-bodied women, 87 aged sick men, 138 aged and sick women, and 149 children under sixteen. In the New Year, though, matters began to improve again: unemployment fell in February, March and April 1864 and by May the number without any work was down to 9,399. Furthermore, by the second half of 1864 there were signs that the war in America was slowly and painfully drawing to a close. Increasing amounts of raw cotton were being procured from sources unconnected with America, and the cotton trade itself was reviving.

In July 1864 the situation had improved to the extent that the sewing school for girls in Fishergate closed as more jobs became available, and the numbers being relieved by the Guardians fell sharply. In August a number of mills reopened with new machinery, having invested in re-equipment during the years of closure. Most people in Preston now believed that the suffering was coming to an end. Inevitably, the progress was not smooth – a sudden increase in unemployment during September 1864 followed the unexpected closure of three mills, and by the end of October some 11,112 people were reportedly out of work. Yet the stocks of raw cotton lying in the Liverpool warehouses were reported to be double the amount in September 1863, and almost four times the quantity stored in September 1862. With more cotton becoming available at reduced prices, the financial position of individual firms was causing great uncertainty. Speculation was rife and many millowners were not prepared to purchase quantities of stock until prices settled. Manufacturers expected prices to drop even further, so preferred to close their mills for a while rather than incur a possible loss. Eventually, though, a gradual settling of prices brought stability to the industry. In the new year of 1865, cotton production steadily increased in Preston and by mid-March, unemployment had fallen to 8,647 people. On 9 April 1865 the news came that the American Civil War had ended. Whether or not the war was the direct and primary cause of the Cotton Famine, this news was psychologically crucial. It meant that there was hope, optimism and an expectation of rapid revival.

Within a month, the mills of Horrocks, Miller & Co. had extended production to 5½ days a week, and at Haslam Brothers mill in Parker Street, which was destroyed by fire in 1860 but rebuilt and equipped with new machinery, it was announced that work would resume imminently. Humber & Son recommenced operations at their Marsh Lane mill, closed since 1862, Hawkins' Greenbank mill reopened for work, as did the Kent Street establishment of Smith and Grime (stopped for eighteen months) and Richard Threlfall & Son offered employment at the Broomfield mill off North Road, closed for well over three years.

As each mill resumed normal production, and the operatives returned to work, the need for stone-breaking or for work on the Moor came to an end. Yet these projects had a lasting legacy for Preston, its people and its townscape. Among the remarkable achievements of those destitute men, the workers during the Cotton Famine, was the remodelling of large tracts of land in and around Preston. To the north, the rough uncultivated Preston Moor was drained and levelled, creating what is known today as Moor Park. A comparable scheme created Avenham and Miller Parks. Preparation work for the cattle market site in Brook Street was completed by these men, and the new workhouse in Watling Street Road was started. The Marsh estate was drained and excavated by these shilling-a-day labourers and in January 1864 the North of England Railway and Carriage Company purchased 60,000 square yards of the recently improved land for a mere twopence per square yard (with the exception of 3,600 square yards, which was sold for a penny halfpenny per square yard). In later years this company became one of the mainstays of Preston's commercial and manufacturing sector, the celebrated Dick Kerr's tramcar works – then English Electric, then British Aerospace, and now Alsthoms.

As the Cotton Famine, the worst economic and social crisis in nineteenth-century Lancashire, came to an end, the terrible suffering of the cotton operatives was acknowledged. William Ewart Gladstone, chancellor of the exchequer 1859–65, and future Prime Minister, and himself a Lancashire man, said in 1866 that 'They knew that the source of their distress lay in the war, yet they never uttered or entertained the wish that any effort should be made to put an end to it, as they held it to be a war for justice and for freedom'. During the American Civil War itself, Abraham Lincoln had also praised the devotion of the Lancashire workmen to the Federal cause, as 'An instance of sublime Christian heroism which has not been surpassed in any age or Country'.

The reality was rather different – many Lancashire people, dependent as they were upon cotton, supported the Confederate cause with enthusiasm, and the plight of the Southern slaves was far from the most important consideration in their thinking. But then, knowing what we know about the circumstances of the Preston cotton workers in the century before the Cotton Famine, they maybe felt that the situation there was not all that different very much closer to home.

Sources and bibliography

Anthony Hewitson, *History of Preston* (Preston Chronicle, 1883)

Peter Whittle, *History of Preston* (1821)

Charles Hardwick, *History of the Borough of Preston* (1857)

Edwin Waugh, *Home Life of the Lancashire factory folk during the Cotton Famine* (Simpkin, Marshall & Co., 1867)

Charles Hardwick, *History of the Preston Strikes*

Catherine Rees, *Locked Out* (Harris Library, 1992)

Margaret Burscough, *The Horrockses, Cotton Kings of Preston* (Carnegie, 2004)

H. I. Dutton and J. E. King, *Ten per cent and No Surrender: The Preston strike 1853–1854* (Cambridge University Press)

The Barefoot Aristocrats: A History of the Amalgamated Association of Operative Cotton Spinners (George Kelsall, 1987)

Preston and the Cotton Industry, vols 1 and 2 (History Group, Curriculum Development Centre, Harris Library)

William Dodd, *The Factory System Illustrated*

William Turner, *Riot! The Story of the East Lancashire Loom Breakers in 1826* (Lancashire County Books, 1992)

G. D. H. Cole and Raymond Postgate, *The Common People 1746–1946* (Methuen, 1946)

T. C. Dickinson, *Cotton Mills of Preston: The Power Behind the Thread* (Carnegie, 2002)

Michael Bush, *The Casualties of Peterloo* (Carnegie, 2005)

David Hunt, *A History of Preston* (Carnegie, 1992, 2008)

Derek Beattie, *A History of Blackburn* (Carnegie, 2007)

Newspapers

The Preston Pilot

Preston Chronicle

Preston Guardian

Other newspapers and journals

The Times

The Builder

Leeds Mercury

The Morning Post

The Leader

The Working Man's Companion

The Daily News

Nonconformist